ADVANCE PRAISE FOR *A PIECE OF PEACE*

"This book is a pleasure to read. It is a great combination of personal experience and street-smart advice including some very potent lifestyle changes. The author draws upon diverse scenarios and situations and has a wonderful ability to connect everything with a common thread, so the continuity is seamless. What is also visible is vulnerability and deep inner strength. It then segues into very practical tips to stay healthy, physically and mentally, during the pandemic and culminates in sage advice to authors. I would highly recommend this book to people from all walks of life, and I'm confident that it will prove to be of immense benefit to anyone interested in achieving a state of healthy physical, intellectual, and spiritual well-being."

~ **Nitin P. Ron, MD, Speaker, Expedition Leader, and Assistant Professor of Clinical Pediatrics**

"*A Piece of Peace* is a wonderful collection of Sweta's reflections on her journey to healing from chronic illness. Sweta's bravery and determination to heal is reflected in her words of wisdom, which I am sure many will find empowering. I loved reading this easy-to-follow guide; it is beautifully honest and packed with tips for every day. Thank you for sharing your inspiring journey."

~ **Mita Mistry, Columnist, mindfulness-based cognitive therapist and acupuncturist**

"What did Sweta Vikram do after a miraculous recovery from near death? She wrote this healing guide to long-term health for your creative mind, body, and soul. Linger a while with her book and let your body unwind and find peace of mind—the keys to setting your creative soul free."

~ **Cauvery Madhavan, author of *The Tainted***

"*A Piece of Peace* by Sweta Vikram is the book every woman needs to have by her bedside. Each chapter is a little piece of magic that is easy to digest after a long day. We can see ourselves in her stories and also gain greater insights into the expectations about a woman's role in our dysfunctional society. She guides us with ease from the lows of experiencing health problems, writer's block, and pandemic survival to the highs of loving deeply and stepping into our own power and spirituality. When times are hard, we just need to know that other women feel the same, as a form of self-empathy. I think every woman will see herself in this book and be glad to have read each juicy page."

~ **Amy Wheeler, Director of Training at Optimal State Yoga Therapy School & Former President of the Board of Directors at International Association of Yoga Therapists**

"*A Piece of Peace* is a chronicle of events related to Vikram's illness and her triumphant return to life. She shares lessons learned on her way to recovery and imparts valuable advice to her readers that can be both life-changing and life-saving. Her story demonstrates the victory of valiance over despair. This is a timely read, especially, because many of us are in low spirits due to the Coronavirus."

~ *The Think Club*, **reviewed by Anil Shrivastava 'Musafir'**

"The recipe for being your most creative and productive self is in this book. Through Sweta's journey of survival she shares the power of mindful living, the value of Ayurvedic healing and how to be the best version of yourself. *A Piece of Peace* is a must-have for your bookshelf."

~ **Paula Rizzo, Author,** *Listful Living: A List-Making Journey to a Less Stressed You*

A PIECE *of* PEACE

Everyday Mindfulness to
Improve Your Well-being and Creativity

SWETA VIKRAM

Loving Healing Press

Ann Arbor, MI

A Piece of Peace: Everyday Mindfulness You Can Use

ISBN 978-1-61599-597-4 paperback
ISBN 978-1-61599-598-1 hardcover
ISBN 978-1-61599-599-8 eBook

Audiobook edition available on Audible.com and iTunes

Published by
Loving Healing Press
5145 Pontiac Trail
Ann Arbor, MI 48105

www.LHPress.com
info@LHPress.com

DEDICATION

For my husband, Anudit

Thank you for believing that I would not just survive but thrive again. Also, for forever mocking my *ghee*-obsession.

Also by Sweta Srivastava Vikram

POETRY

Kaleidoscope: An Asian Journey with Colors

Because All is Not Lost: Verse on Grief

Beyond the Scent of Sorrow

No Ocean Here: Stories in Verse about Women from Asia, Africa, and the Middle East

Wet Silence: Poems about Hindu Widows

Saris and a Single Malt

FICTION

Louisiana Catch

Perfectly Untraditional

Contents

Introduction

I was on the cancer watch list until recently because of my chronic illness. When I showed up for my screening, a nurse at the surgeon's office said, "I believe chronic illness in women stems from unresolved trauma." Her words stayed with me. The ancient wisdom of Ayurveda, *knowledge of life*, also teaches us that total well-being needs our mind, body, and spirit to be in sync.

According to the US National Library of Medicine, National Institutes of Health, chronic diseases are among the most prevalent and costly health conditions in the United States. Nearly half (approximately 45%, or 133 million) of all Americans suffer from at least one chronic disease[1], and the number is growing. In fact, persistent conditions are the nation's leading cause of death and disability.

Unless you live or have lived with a chronic illness, you don't know how debilitating it can be. Your body doesn't feel like your own. It takes up space and makes everything more difficult. On some days, you can hike ten miles; on other days, you don't have the energy to make yourself a cup of tea. Sometimes, it morphs into an unrecognizable mess. Sometimes, it belittles you. You might appear fine to the world while writhing in pain on the inside. When chronic illness flares up, it impacts your mental health, too. Every follow-up visit to the doctor or surgeon's office can trigger your trauma.

Chronic illness changes the quality of your life. When you know that your body can betray you any moment, trust becomes difficult. Simple things that were accessible one night ago start to seem distant. You feel life is happening to you and people do things to you. It's

---

[1]https://www.ncbi.nlm.nih.gov/pmc/articles/PMC5876976/#B3-ijerph-15-00431

easy to personalize every word and action. It's easy to feel like a victim. But then one does become a victim, no? You didn't ask to be sick. You don't deserve the pain. But you see seasons pass by and life go on for others, and you are stuck in limbo. Every day feels different. Every day, your body feels different.

Here is something else I have observed: because chronic illness is often invisible and people can't see physical signs and symptoms (some choose not to see it), they assume how you feel. The thing with chronic illness is that you can look perfect on the outside but feel bruised and depleted on the inside. And people gauge your health by your appearance. I constantly hear, "You look great. Everything must be good," instead of "How are you doing?" Some even start to suggest that you might be making it up and will offer unsolicited and unhelpful advice. Sometimes they pretend that the illness doesn't exist, and they want you to go along with it.

What do you say when people have already made up their minds?

Pay attention to your mental and physical wellness. Do not correlate the severity of your symptoms with your need to voice your opinion. Not everything has to be measured and judged on a scale of 1 to 10. You didn't do this to yourself. Every single person I have spoken with, who has a chronic illness, has said one thing: it changed them forever.

I wrote this book to empower your personal and professional life. This is by sharing how I use practical daily doses of mindfulness and Ayurveda, Ayurveda is a practice which customizes preventative wellness to the unique constitution of every individual. Don't wait to take action after you have fallen ill. I also wrote it to remind you that the quality of your life changes when you start to look inward for strength, instead of relying on others. Surround yourself with good people; stand in your truth; and don't apologize for your voice. Self-care and mindfulness are revolutionary and not optional for your healing and creativity.

This book is for everybody, particularly those suffering from chronic health conditions and navigating life, passion, and responsibilities. There is nothing inherently limiting it to writers. For instance, the essay on financial security for writing also applies to other creative pursuits, and what I say about meditation or eating attitudes applies to everyone regardless of how they spend their time or what they pursue professionally. You will see that certain themes and messages run through the book, and I apply them in a cyclical pattern in various circumstances to help with various issues: chronic ill health, the profession of writing as a case study in creativity, and coping with the pandemic.

In hindsight, my illness and everything leading up to it feels like a blessing in disguise. It's changed how I experience time, relationships, creativity, and the world at large. I know who matters in my life and where my honesty is respected. My energy and attention are reserved for those who deserve it. I have learned to prioritize myself on a daily basis. It's given me *a piece of peace*.

But, please, note that the content in this book is purely informative and educational in nature and should not be construed as medical advice. The information isn't intended to diagnose, treat, mitigate, cure, or prevent any disease. If you have a medical condition, please consult a health professional. Speak with your physician before making changes to your diet or routine.

REFLECTIONS

A year-long journaling of my thoughts

SEPTEMBER 2018: Reflections from the Hospital Room
Last morning, I didn't think I would make it. I have rarely known fear. I said it to my husband and my doctor cousin, who has been our biggest strength in these times, "I thought I wouldn't make it." But I made it to today.

I woke up exactly at the time of my birth. What does that mean? I don't know! But I do know that life happens when we are busy planning it. Who knew that after attending a colleague's book launch in Maryland, I would board the train and my life would change forever? This past weekend and upcoming week were supposed to be full—my niece's upcoming first birthday party, the tickets for the Global Citizens Festival, my first self-care webinars for writers, my first board meeting, and a trip to Chicago to do an event at Mango Pickle for my novel, *Louisiana Catch*. Instead, I ended up in the emergency room with severe complications. My regular doctor was away, so we found an Indian doctor, clad in a sari, who was available and affectionately said, "Goddess Durga will take care of you," the words my mom would always say.

The docs are still figuring out what's going on. In my heart I know what started it. I had begun to fall sick toward the end of our Europe trip the previous month.. The docs are still shocked at the symptoms I present because I am a pretty fit, grounded, and healthy person otherwise.

As I stare at the sunrise from my hospital room this morning, I have vowed to build better personal boundaries. It might annoy some people. Takers don't know when to stop because we, the givers, enable them. But this isn't about me pushing people away; it's about me taking better care of myself.

I want to thank everyone who has reached out and offered help and prayers and hugs. Thank you to my clients and colleagues for being so incredibly supportive! I am not able to respond to texts or inbox messages right away, or take phone calls right now—the meds and all of this are exhausting. But know that I appreciate you, and I promise to respond to everyone in due course.

OCTOBER 2018: There is a huge difference between physical and emotional pain when it comes to creativity. They both make us vulnerable and there is a sense of grief, loss, and betrayal. But they tap into different sides of our brain. When my mom passed away, I wrote a poetry collection, *Saris and a Single Malt*, inside of a week. In these past five weeks of being sick, and still searching for answers and praying for healing, I haven't written a single word. I have tried, but nothing. Honestly, I have been feeling frustrated. What do you call a writer who doesn't write? And then out of nowhere, this surprise care package got delivered. It's from one of the readers and fans of *Louisiana Catch*. Her card says that the book helped her heal and that she couldn't wait for my next novel. Just when I was ready to give up on the universe, it showed me a sign.

I was feeling bummed out today—this is the first *Dussehra* in my adult life where I am not cooking up a storm and sharing food with loved ones. No colorful clothes, no recreating Mom's recipes, nothing festive at all. This is the first *Dussehra* of my life where I am grappling for a slice of the ordinariness of our daily lives—something that we so often take for granted. Running between doctor appointments, swimming through unknown waters, and feeling agonized with the status quo, I was greeted by an extremely well-mannered and pleasant Uber driver. He told me he had been in Kolkata, India, caring for a sick family member. In India, Kolkata is the land of *Dussehra* celebrations and Indian sweets. The driver was Bangladeshi. He took six months off work and moved to Bangladesh for this person, then back to India. Things eventually got better, and he returned to the United States. When I asked him if the break was scary, he said that he got back to driving Uber and he is still one of Uber's highly recommended drivers. Lesson learned: there will be many more Dussehras to celebrate if there is health and healing. A break does not necessarily mean an end; it can mean a pause.

NOVEMBER 2018: Last evening, on the way back from my doctor's appointment, there were no cabs available, and Uber had a long wait period because of the snowstorm. A fellow New Yorker noticed I was unwell and asked if I needed help. She literally held me by my shoulders and helped me cross the street until we had avoided all the slush. Humanity thrives even in today's times. This past week has been a lot. To those hurting, "I see you. I believe in you. You are strong. You matter. You are valid. You are believed. You are supported."

When your life stands still and your breath doesn't sound like your own—in all of this, a reader sends you a note that her mother wants you to get well soon because she is done reading *Louisiana Catch* and wants to read your next book. So long as there is life, there will be challenges. Instead of getting despondent about what's not working out and things being difficult, believe there is something better waiting for you.

DECEMBER 2018: I made it. The surgery, though complicated, went alright. Surviving is a beautiful thing because it teaches you who and what matter most. I had told a few people that if I made it to Christmas, I would like to go up to some place where we could really have a white Christmas—snow, Santa, hot chocolate, and lots of Christmas carols. This morning, I woke up at home. Not snowy, not white. But this morning, I woke up. This morning, I woke up and saw the lights on our Christmas tree. This morning, I woke up and felt my breath on my hands. How often we take our breath for granted. Thank you life, for reminding me of the smallest ways in which we can experience a miracle.

JANUARY 2019: Today, after a week, I was able to step outside the house. Today, after months, I climbed a few subway stairs—a test run. I was slow and my legs were all shaky. And I am normally one who, always in a rush, holds a green juice in one hand and says, "Excuse me," as I run up the escalator. But getting a second chance at life also takes away all your unnecessary fears, stress, and pressure. I was OK with being slow today. I was OK with asking for help. Keep in mind, where you are today isn't your final destination. This isn't how your story will end. Sending a big hug and a virtual cup of chai to everyone who is healing, hurting, or figuring this thing called life. You are not alone!

Today I walked to get a haircut in honor of my birthday. In the scheme of all the awesome things people are doing in this world, this might sound like nothing. But I am feeling so grateful. The same legs that prepped for the half marathon and yoga teacher training and 12-mile hikes and all the crazy dance workouts couldn't move with ease for months. But two days before my birthday, they carried me for 1.5 miles, without complaint, and reminded me that healing is just as real as falling sick. Believe in yourself. Believe in the healing power of your own body.

FEBRUARY 2019: Light is on the other side of your scars. When people tell me it's too cold to step out, I smile. I have been home since September. I have touched windowpanes to feel the change in season since I missed experiencing end of summer fun, autumn boot swag, and the year-end holiday festivities. Trust me; I would give anything to go out in the bat of an eye. But these past few months have taught me that life happens when you are busy planning it. You can't orchestrate your every move. That is why it is so important to live each moment fully because you never know what tomorrow holds for you. Throw away the fears, the anger, the hurt, the disappointments, the heartaches, the judgments, the inhibitions, or whatever else that is weighing you down. This moment, this breath, that's all you have for sure. CELEBRATE IT. Celebrate you. Celebrate life.

This week, for the first time since I'd ended up in the ER, I took the subway by myself. It's been over five months, and I was a little afraid. But my husband and friends and cousins reminded me that if I can fight for my life, I can handle anything. I was the slowest on the stairs and the last one to step outside the subway car. Got off at the wrong stop and wondered how much the neighborhood had changed in five months. I was so exhausted from the short commute that I took a short nap during lunch. I know I have miles to go and my healing is months away, but for this week, these baby steps were enough. Healing takes time and courage.

For the first time since September 2018, I was able to cook an entire meal today. Nothing fancy. And, sure, it took me hours—between rest and breaks and managing pain and seeking my sous-chef husband's help, and finally getting in a nap—to make *Tehri* (North Indian rice and vegetable dish—threw in the "masala" egg for protein) and *saag* (sautéed mustard greens and spinach in garlic and other spices). If you know me, you probably know that I love to cook and entertain. But falling sick suddenly changed everything. For months, I couldn't even get up to drink a glass of water, and struggled with breathing, never mind cooking or grocery shopping or entertaining. But today, I was able to cook! So what if it took me a really LONG time to prepare this meal? It is still a small, positive change in the healing journey. Gratitude for these miraculous moments.

MARCH 2019: It's a gorgeous day in New York City today. I was able to go for a walk by myself in the sun. I touched some flowers; took pictures of barren trees; smiled at dogs; listened to podcasts (a few of them). The breeze touched my face, and it felt amazing. I wanted to tell every pedestrian on the sidewalk how blessed they are to experience all of this. But I didn't because I didn't want to be the cray-cray lady. Hahaha. The simple things that were inaccessible for six months are becoming available again—even if in small quantities. My heart is full, and I am reminded instantly what a gift it is to be alive.

Here is my friendly advice to anyone who identifies as a woman: stop relying on people to build you up. Stop giving away your power. Instead of seeking outside validation and approval, focus on staying authentic and building your own path. It might feel lonely at first, but you will find your tribe. When a woman stands up for herself, she inspires other women to speak for themselves.

This *Holi*, festival of colors, we are eating our home-cooked colors (and loving them!) instead of playing with them. Brussel sprouts in glazed soy sauce and ginger, butternut squash sautéed in South Indian spices, wild rice cooked with a small amount of stir-fried Korean chicken, *saag*, olives marinated in Middle Eastern spices, sunny-side-up eggs, and guacamole—all organic. No grains. No dairy. No gluten. No added sugar. As the wise say, "The food you eat can be either the safest and most powerful form of medicine or the slowest form of poison."

APRIL 2019: It is so bloody scary to rebuild your body, strength, career, and life from scratch. These past few months have been such a diligent teacher. It's taught me things about myself and my ecosystem that I am beyond grateful for. It's reminded me that when you stop fighting the status quo and allow yourself the time to heal, the body reciprocates the love. That said, I will never take a single breath for granted. I will never take a single word that leaves my pen as a given.

We are in the Windy City to celebrate the one-year anniversary of *Louisiana Catch*. Best gift: the Uber driver says, "You could be the next female Tony Robbins," and a 7-year-old interviewed me about my writing process and creativity tips.

GOT INVITED TO ONE OF THE BIGGEST CONFERENCES FOR WOMEN! I'm still shaking with joy and in a happy shock! The one thing that haunted me the most when I fell critically ill: feeling invisible. My identity had become my illness. All well-meaning suggestions were about my physical well-being and healing. Getting out of my comfort zone and choosing vulnerability because as Brené Brown, an American professor, lecturer, author, and podcast host, once said, "Vulnerability sounds like truth and feels like courage."

You grow where your energy goes. Be very mindful of what you feed your mind.

Your dreams should scare you and make you work harder. Because if they don't, they are not big enough.

Scarcity mindset helps no one. Invite abundance. Share. Learn. Build a community. Stay positive.

Not everyone will understand your journey, and that is OK. But if you don't believe in yourself and don't take action to create opportunities, nothing will ever change for the better.

MAY 2019: My first international trip since I fell ill. Such a strange feeling, landing in the same city on Mother's Day where my mom passed away five years ago—New Delhi! I bought her favorite Christian Dior lipstick from duty-free and intend to wear it all day today in her honor.

It's scary to put yourself out there. Yesterday, I walked into a room full of men and there was absolute silence as I spoke about mindset and Ayurveda coaching and how it can transform their lives. Three quarters of the way through the conversation, a gentleman entrepreneur said, "I would pay for your coaching. Respect your knowledge. It makes total sense. You should also give a talk to raise awareness." All the other men chimed in, "This is powerful work." BEST PART: my Dad was in that room when this conversation transpired, and once we got home, he said, "It was amazing to see how everyone responded to you. We should have taken a photo." My father held my hands when I couldn't walk, massaged my head in the middle of the night when sleep eluded me, and made *khichadi* (a traditional rice and lentil dish) when I was ill and could barely eat. He reminded me every day to have a positive mindset—how key it was to my own healing. I heard him pray every morning for my recovery—even though my dad isn't a religious man. I would look at Instagram food videos and say, "Papa, can we please eat ALL of this when I get better and visit India?" To be able to eat, breathe, move, smile, and sleep—such gifts. I will never take them for granted. So grateful to be celebrating resilience, positivity, and my second lease on life. As Roy T. Bennet wrote: "Life is about accepting the challenges along the way, choosing to keep moving forward, and savoring the journey."

JUNE 2019: I've progressed from crawling in pain to being housebound for months to using a wheelchair to actually doing a high intensity workout four days in a row As Janice Trachtman wrote in *Catching What Life Throws at You*: "Everything is within your power, and your power is within you." Today, for the first time in nine months, I was able to use my favorite equipment at the gym. I like my workouts just as much as I love writing. I was terrified at first but mostly grateful. It's just wonderful, being able to move naturally again. I kept playing the Bollywood song *Apna Time Aayegaa* ("My Time Will Come") on loop. This was the song I listened to when I couldn't walk. This was the song I cried to on days hope didn't want to befriend me. This was the song I whispered to my body when I took my first step after months of being homebound. Never give up faith, friends. I hear you. I see you.

Pain has been my greatest teacher. The one consistent question my surgeon and physician and some friends have asked over the past few months: "Sweta, how did you not get depressed despite nearly dying and losing everything?" My answer: "The resilience and mental strength come from my workouts." Movement and exercise contribute positively to our mental health. They teach us to cope with our physical and emotional pain. They remind us that our today isn't a representation of our tomorrow. They reiterate, be mindful of what you put in your body—both food and thoughts. They lower stress.

How about you? Have exercise and movement made a difference to your life?

JULY 2019: In case you needed this reminder today, according to J,K. Rowling: "Happiness can be found even in the darkest of times, if one only remembers to turn on the light." A positive attitude gives you control over your circumstances versus the circumstances controlling you. Did you know that positive thinking can impact your physical, emotional, and mental health? It can even increase your lifespan, lower stress, and improve the quality of your relationships. BUT, how do you stay positive on days when everything feels low and demoralizing?

Three simple things I remind my clients of every week (hope they help you too):

1. It is not your job to make everyone happy.

2. Pay attention to the people around you—are they bringing you down or lifting you up?

3. Self-care isn't selfish—you can't serve others from an empty space.

AUGUST 2019: When you are kinder toward yourself, you are more compassionate toward others.

It's OK to admit you are feeling exhausted.

It's OK to not take a phone call.

It's OK to prioritize yourself.

It's OK to cancel a commitment.

It's OK to not feel exuberant all the time.

It's OK to carve out "me-time."

It's OK to not be OK at times.

The day I was admitted to the ER, a very dear friend's husband was admitted, too. I made it out alive, but he didn't. When she needed me, I was bedridden; when I needed her, she was making his funeral arrangements. That's how unpredictable life can be. In case you are struggling to feel grateful today and wondering why things are feeling rough, remember, if you are reading this, you are still alive. Focusing on what you have (including your breath) versus what you don't can make all the difference. As Jon Kabat-Zinn wrote, "Even if you are on your deathbed, as long as you are breathing, there is more right with you than wrong with you."

SEPTEMBER 2019: Difficult roads, challenging times, and vulnerability can lead to beautiful destinations if you work hard and stay true to your path without competing or complaining. I know how quickly and suddenly everything can be taken away, including your own breath. So, I plan to celebrate small and big moments and learn from hard times but not become hard times.

When you are forced to restart your life from scratch, you lose fear, ego, and expectations. What a scary yet humbling and beautiful feeling to be a beginner. Brené Brown wrote, "The willingness to show up changes us, it makes us a little braver each time." The higher the resentment, the lower the self-care. If you want peace and calm and contentment and growth in your life, learn to fall in love with imperfections. I am not suggesting turning into a slob, leaving crusty dishes in your sink, or having dirty laundry strewn all over the floor. I mean, if you can love your own messy, flawed self, you will be open to accepting others with human flaws. This simple transformation can lower your expectations of others and in turn reduce your stress, thus improving the quality of your relationships.

LESSONS LEARNED

"Sometimes the bravest and most important
thing you can do is just show up."

~ Brené Brown

Unhealed Emotional Trauma Manifests in Our Body As Disease

I was told that my illness may have been influenced by things that happened to me and not because of something I did or did not do. I witnessed a crime in 2013. There was no flight or fight; I froze. I was so shattered by what I had witnessed in what was supposed to have been my "safe space" that I couldn't move or speak or react. I was also scared. Was I safe around a perpetrator whom no one suspected but I had caught in the act? I felt deeply shamed for my inability to act in the moment.

I kept agonizing over the incident so badly that I didn't want to believe my recall. I was angry at myself for being present. I felt even more upset at my memory that held every detail together. Why couldn't I forget?

My body started to break down slowly, and I started to fall sick frequently. I became an emotional wreck who was triggered in the most unexpected of places. PTSD became my middle name—nightmares, flashbacks, and triggering thoughts. I knew that I had to speak up for my own sanity and well-being.

It took me a few years to muster the courage to share what had happened. I was nervous and queasy. I didn't understand at the time that most people would rather not know the truth. Given that I teach yoga and mindfulness to survivors of sexual assault and domestic violence, I know that victims and survivors aren't always believed. I didn't know that the same bias would be extended to me, a witness.

No one asked how I was doing. Or why it took me three years to voice my biggest nightmare. How that one incident forever changed my life—no questions about it. I was threatened and almost ostracized by those I had held closest. While I was called names and was accused of lying, the perpetrator got sympathy. I felt completely broken and alone. Anger and betrayal engulfed me. The stress and trauma took over my body.

Research studies show that stressful events are common before the onset of many chronic illnesses. My trauma had occurred in October 2013. In September 2016, I started to face the repercussions for naming the perpetrator. In September 2018, I was in the ER, fighting for my life, and eventually found out that I had to live with a full-blown chronic illness. Trauma and chronic disease are linked by common patterns that evolve over years.

Will I Ever Write Again? Surviving My Worst Fears As a Writer

It was the morning of Thursday, September 20, 2018. I was in the train, headed back home to NYC from Maryland, after doing the introduction and in-author conversation at a colleague's book launch the night before.

Exactly 40 days ago, on August 7, I had won the Voices of the Year Award (previous recipients include Chelsea Clinton and founders of Women's March) for my debut U.S. novel, *Louisiana Catch*, and work with female survivors of violence. A few months prior to that, I was invited at Twitter, NYC to be a part of a discussion about the role of social media in bringing about social change. The female protagonist, Ahana, in *Louisiana Catch* uses social media to raise awareness about violence against women and organize a global, feminist conference. It was like my real world and fictional world had collided at the crossroads of creation.

None of this fell into my lap. I worked very hard and was published by a small press. A lot of meticulous planning and partnership with my publisher had gone into the book launch. So, after 8–10 hectic months of working nonstop—managing my company, doing the book launch and tour, going to school, and juggling an enriching but demanding personal life—my husband and I took a trip to Central Europe, which we had been planning for years. We spent three weeks in August hiking, playing tourist, learning about history, visiting museums, and exploring delicious meals across multiple nations. After we returned from Europe, I headed to India for work in early September and made it back in time for my colleague's book launch. 2018 felt like the year of magic and checking items off my bucket list.

I felt both grateful for and inspired by all the good that had happened. I wasn't going to waste time in a moving train. So, I used the opportunity to write down plans for the upcoming months. I was supposed to resume the book tour for *Louisiana Catch* by the end of September. Bookstores and/or book clubs in Boston, Baton Rouge, Chicago, San Francisco, Seattle, and India were on the list of places I was scheduled to travel to. A few book clubs even offered to cook

elaborate meals based off the Indian-Cajun culinary theme in
Louisiana Catch. I was scheduled to teach webinars to writers and
bring creativity and wellness together in a classroom in India at a
writing retreat. All these years of hard work had paid off and 2018
was continuing to dole out surprises.

The ticket inspector broke my reverie. After I handed my ticket to
him, I dived into a bag of dates my colleague had packed for me as
snack. As I looked out the train window and munched on the dates,
my mind kept going in so many different directions, including the
theme of my next novel. What I didn't know at the time was that life
was returning the favor and making plans of its own. All of a sudden,
I started to feel unwell. I must have been an hour or 1.5 hours from
Penn Station, NYC, when I texted my husband (fortunately he was
working from home that day) that something was wrong, and I
couldn't explain. We went over what I had eaten. This was only
home-cooked meals in the past few days—on the day of the book
launch, I finished dinner by 5:30 pm. And instead of wine, I drank a
turmeric latte because I was jetlagged and exhausted. I had practiced
yoga before catching the train to NYC. And after masala chai in the
morning, dates were my mid-morning snack. Between healthy meals
and workouts, I couldn't fathom what was causing the uneasiness.

I somehow made it home. But everything went south from there.
First, it was a fever; then terrible stomach pain; then I couldn't walk
or breathe or eat. My husband took me to the ER. The next thing we
knew, I was in the ER all night. The only thing I understood was the
shock in the doctors' voices at how unwell I was—shock at how none
of it made sense given I ate healthy, worked out 6 days a week,
practiced/taught 6-8 hours of yoga every week, and was fit. Or at
least looked really fit. How could I be so sick?

When I was in the hospital room alone, I started to make notes on
my phone. Writing is how I make sense of the world. Writing is a
form of meditation. Writing helps me heal. And I figured that writing
about the suddenness and severity of my illness would lessen my
trauma. As the wise say, "Every secret of a writer's soul, every
experience of his life, every quality of his mind, is written large in his
works."

Once I got home, I continued planning my book tour. There was
no reason to believe otherwise. The doctors thought I would be okay
after two weeks of antibiotics. But life is the biggest leveler. Slowly,
my health started to deteriorate. As the doctors ran tests and MRIs

and scans, my body turned frailer by the day. I couldn't eat or sleep or get out of the house. Needless to say, my yoga and meditation practice suffered. I turned to my notebook, books, and laptop but I was too weak and in too much pain to write or read. Between the pain and the medication, my eyesight became weak.

No matter how many books you write or awards you win, most of us creative professionals suffer from FOMO, also known as the fear of missing out. I missed out on every literary event, readings, literary festival, book launch, etc. I missed writing. And people suggesting "Now that you are home, work on your next novel," didn't help either. I fought with myself: how did I manage to write a collection of poems, *Saris and a Single Malt*, inside of a week after my mom died? How could I not write now that I was in pain all over again? What did this break mean? Could I even call myself a writer if I wasn't writing?

I didn't know where to look for answers. After months of probing, prodding, and everything excruciating, we found out that I needed surgery. I will spare you the details of what happened to me. Emotional pain, though still hurtful, can lead to some incredible creative bursts—they first hurt but eventually heal. But that's not true for debilitating physical pain. You can't focus on writing when you can barely breathe.

One night, over dinner, my husband asked why I wasn't writing again now that I believed I had the mental strength to get back to it. I said to him, "I don't know if I can ever write again." Every year, I make a list of writing goals and diligently meet them. But by fall of 2018, I found myself feeling uninspired—an alien feeling to me. In my entire life, I have never been out of ideas. I have written and traditionally published 12 books in 9 years. He looked at me. "Why don't you practice what you teach your students and clients? Sit with your laptop and wait for the words. Repeat every day until words happen. This isn't about a 'dry spell' as much as it is about inertia."

Honestly, I am not always receptive to spousal feedback on my creative process. But... something about my husband's suggestions stayed with me. I saw the sincerity in his eyes. And I had no better ideas to get out of my funk. While meditating that night, I went back to my yoga teachings; they reiterate that if we can't control our situation, we need to adjust our attitude. Yes, my life is not where I'd like it to be. But the universe has been kind and I am alive. *Louisiana*

Catch was a success, and I couldn't be more grateful for all the love it's received, including a Pushcart Prize nomination.

This morning, by 8:30 am, I sat with my laptop on my lap, determined to write. No new ideas for a novel or poetry book trickled down. Of course, I checked Facebook, Instagram, Twitter, LinkedIn, WhatsApp, and some YouTube workout videos and funky recipes for when I can cook epic things again. A friend or two called, and I let the conversation go on for too long. There were other distractions too, including a nap. But, somehow, I kept returning to this essay. Instead of my usual two hours, it's taken me an entire day to write it. But it's now complete. I managed to break my shackles of the fear "Will I Ever Write Again?"

I know that I am not alone—in that, so many of us have been tested, and endured times when writing feels furthest from us. The fears and insecurities can make us question our very own identity as writers. But here is what I've learned: No one can help you but you yourself. Don't expect a masterpiece on day one. But keep at it. When you show up with dedication and devotion, your words do, too. The Taj Mahal wasn't built in a day.

How Yoga Has Taught Me to Accept My Extroverted-Introvert Self

"Blessed are those who do not fear solitude, who are not afraid of their own company, who are not always desperately looking for something to do, something to amuse themselves with, something to judge."
~ Paulo Coelho, *Manuscript Found in Accra*

In October 2019, when I was visiting India, I had an interesting conversation with my father.

My dad, who is in his 70s, is still active, bright, and involved in his work. He travels extensively and is inspiring in many ways. But when I said to him that he needs to put his phone away every now and then, quieten his mind, and connect with his inner voice, he said to me, "That is the one thing I don't think is possible. What if someone needs something urgent? And anyway, I don't think anyone can make their mind quiet."

I jokingly said, "Papa, you don't run an emergency service. It's okay to disconnect. Meditation can help you create the quiet space in your mind." The thought that haunted me that day: *how can a country give the gift of yoga and Ayurveda to the world, but its own citizens not embrace its benefits?*

The concept of stillness and calm doesn't elude just my father. In India—where I spent a big part of my life growing up—I rarely saw anyone alone or quiet. Whether at a gym, corner store, salon or restaurant, from pedestrian paths to private homes, people are always surrounded by people. I have rarely witnessed silence between words. Even today, in homes, airports, airplanes, or trains… if people aren't arguing or excessively talking about Bollywood, politics, cricket, familial gossip, or TV shows, they are loudly watching WhatsApp videos. I have seen both my mother and mother-in-law perform their morning *puja*—brief daily worship rites at home) while simultaneously dishing out advice to the domestic help. But isn't the time of prayer also the time for stillness and meditation? Silence and solitude are frightening to many where I come from.

I have a few close friends and cousins in India who don't thrive on socializing with two dozen folks every weekend or attending a birthday bash at a club every weeknight or showing up to every family get-together. They, and people like them, who like to dwell in their realm of intentional isolation, have been labeled as "antisocial." They are frowned upon and thought of as lacking social etiquette. There are serious negative connotations attached to these people's desire to disconnect with society on occasion. "Loner" is the term hurled at them—like something is inherently wrong with wanting some quiet and alone time.

Honestly, most people aren't allowed the luxury of picking up solitude over social commitments within the culture. You are expected to attend your colleague's grandma's 90th birthday party with the same enthusiasm you'd attend your cousin's baby's thread ceremony—be it a weeknight or a weekend. I remember wedding seasons were exhausting because they meant getting dressed (sometimes on a weeknight), buying gifts, and showing up to events for people you didn't particularly care about. I couldn't wrap my brains around those commitments, but I still brought that thinking with me to the United States when I moved here.

In my early life in the U.S., I emulated the lifestyle I grew up with in India, because people learn from their surroundings and adapt from how they are bought up. This meant people were in and out of our home constantly in New York City. I was cooking and entertaining even on weeknights. Our home was "party central". You'd never see me quiet. You'd never see me alone. You'd never find me sitting. And I took pride in my moniker "social butterfly."

I was probably exhausted from managing a full-time job, graduate school, and a hectic social calendar along with home and family—it showed through my occasional meltdowns. My husband was definitely unhappy about not having any personal space or having his football Sundays overrun with Sunday brunches and happy hours and other innumerable social plans over the weekend. I have to admit, after hectic weekdays at work, my over-scheduled calendar made little room for any personal growth or creative writing in my life, which frustrated me.

But I didn't know better. I didn't have the courage to say no and definitely wanted to fit in. I lived in a world peppered with stereotypes: the number of party invites, the different circles of friends you hung out with, the innovative dishes you brought to the potluck—all defined the barometer of success for socially adept individuals. While my American friends' eyes brightened up when they talked about pajamas and Thai takeout on a Friday evening, as an Indian, if you didn't have plans on a Friday evening or if you weren't trying out new restaurants with friends on a Saturday night, you were deemed a loser.

If your idea of a nice birthday celebration was enjoying a quiet dinner with a few loved ones instead of throwing a wild bash, you were considered unpopular. These were the harsh rules the majority of Indian kids were often brought up with, and I was one of them. These values weren't part of dinner conversations, but they were narrated through action on a daily basis. Remember, in our 20s, most of us cared about external validation and tried to fit into spaces that weren't for us.

But as I got older and yoga became a big part of my life, even off the mat, I found contradictions and discrepancies between who I was expected to be and who I truly was at my core. The real me began to emerge from underneath the rubble. I started to notice that being constantly busy felt inauthentic and empty. I felt the need to refill myself if I had spent my entire day around people. I felt an increasing distance between myself and true happiness. And I am one of those people (truly blessed) who is happy and positive most of the time.

I accepted that I wasn't conscious of the quality of people I surrounded myself with. Don't get me wrong; all my "friends" were graduates from incredible schools, in amazing jobs, and in stable relationships. On paper, they met the criteria any and every parent would have approved. But did we have other things in common aside from our socially approved accolades? Were we even evolving at a similar pace? Some people made me defensive—the ones who didn't understand why writing, activism, coaching, and healing were my chosen career paths, given that I have held jobs with Kellogg's, in the retail industry, and a bank.

It took me a long time to accept that not every relationship nourished me. Because I had never paused and reflected about my own needs, I never asked myself the bigger questions like: if hanging out with certain people angered me or made me feel bad about my life choices, what was the point? Did we want the same things from life or were we too afraid to even ask these questions because unfamiliarity would mean parting ways?

Was this the life I wanted or was this the only life I had always known, so I was afraid to walk away from it? But how could I find the answers to my quandary if I didn't make time for myself in my own life?

Pause and assess. Pause and reflect. Pause and build boundaries—sometimes around my own self. Pause and breathe. Pause and reassess.

The Bhagavad Gita teaches us that "Yoga is the journey of the self, through the self, to the self." I finally understood that while the extrovert in me loves people and enjoys seeing friends and family on a regular basis, the introvert in me is particular about the quality of people I hang out with.

I don't need people to validate my existence or choices. While I thrive on the energy of the people around me, I also love my own company. I get overwhelmed if I have no time to pause and process conversations and interactions. Much as I appreciate social dining, I also occasionally like buying a cup of soup and eating it by myself. I prefer intimate gatherings and deeper, personal connections rather than shallow engagements. Life is too precious to squander away over meaningless interactions.

Yoga has reiterated that alone time to recharge is non-negotiable for me. Writing and teaching yoga and Ayurveda workshops are part of my self-care regime. I need quietude to dive deep into my creative spaces and solitude to connect with my true self. To remain a perpetual learner and student of life, I need a daily dosage of stillness. Yoga has helped me embrace my true self without apologies or anger.

My older niece told me recently that she liked how I lived: happy to order in takeout and watch Netflix with the family on a Saturday night with as much enthusiasm as ready to go to a party or attend a literary event or read a book alone. These events don't define me as a person. For me, that's the most heartfelt compliment I have ever received as an extroverted introvert in my journey of finding myself through stillness and solitude.

How Gratitude Helped Me Stay Alive and Heal

> "Gratitude turns what we have into enough, and more. It turns denial into acceptance, chaos into order, confusion into clarity…it makes sense of our past, brings peace for today, and creates a vision for tomorrow."
>
> —Melody Beattie, *The Language of Letting Go*

I opened my eyes in the hospital and saw a woman throw up violently. It took me a few seconds to grasp my bearings. I was in the recovery room after my surgery. The last thing I remembered from earlier that morning was talking to my surgeon and then waving at my husband, father, and cousin as the nurse took me inside the operating room. I also remembered feeling overwhelmed looking at all the surgical lights and gadgets and telling one of the surgeons, "This is scary, just like in the movies."

The painkillers made me forget for a moment that I had a few invasive surgical cuts. I distinctly remember one of the nurses pointing at the other woman in the recovery room. "Poor thing, she is literally puking her guts out." Apparently, this young woman had had stomach-related surgery and the anesthesia was making her sick. Of course, she was under the influence of painkillers so she couldn't feel the pain from her stitches getting tugged. But I couldn't even imagine how much more painful her recovery would have been.

At the time, I didn't know that my surgery had turned out to be a complicated procedure. Apparently, the surgeon had to step out midway and seek my husband's permission to go ahead with what they had to do next. I was numb from the painkillers and woozy from the anesthesia. But I do remember saying a thank you to the universe. I wasn't reacting to anesthesia; because I had been an otherwise healthy person most of my life, it never occurred to me to check with the surgeon if post-surgery side effects were even a possibility. I kept whispering gratitude and falling asleep again. Even in that drugged moment I remember thinking that gratitude is probably what kept me sane and alive for the four months leading up to the surgery.

In the ER, where I saw my husband and doctor cousin's confused faces as the doctors narrated what was going on, I felt grateful despite the inexplicable pain and chaos. I had family by my side. What were the odds that my husband wasn't traveling for work and my cousin wasn't on call?

When I got home from the hospital, we didn't know my health would take a turn for the worse. I felt like a lab rat on which different specialists were experimenting, in the hope to find out answers. It was a dark period of my life, but I remember saying to my husband, "At least none of this happened when I was doing the book tour or when we were in Europe. Or in India or during the flights." I had spent a lot of time traveling on airplanes to promote my book.

We finally met with a surgeon who believed in the same ethos as us. He was kind, pleasant, and compassionate—qualities extremely important to me. Gratitude is what I felt after our first meeting. What if I had ended up with an aggressive surgeon who wanted to rip out half my organs versus a conservative one who believed in using a combination of surgery and holistic healing? He recommended getting acupuncture post-procedure. I have had friends' doctors tell them that acupuncture, yoga, and Ayurveda are all hogwash.

On low days pre- and post-surgery, gratitude taught me to stay centered. Chronic illness can make you very lonely and aloof. Your life changes overnight. You might still look healthy, but you are in constant pain. You are confined to the house while others go on to live their lives. East coast winter and our premature sunsets can make for depressing moments. I've mentioned before, I remember touching windowpanes to get a feel for the weather. From the end of summer to Groundhog Day, my living room window worked as my weather pal. Gratitude showed me the richness of my life—for close to five months, we had friends and family by our side. It's not easy for anyone to devote so much time and energy to someone else's healing. But I am blessed, because right from the ER to home to back again in the hospital for surgery to recovery after surgery to the holiday season, we had people cheering us on and surrounding us with their time and love.

Gratitude showed me how to focus on the beauty in my life despite my illness. Though the process has been slow, my body is at last healing. I am returning to work and seeing friends. It's taught me to focus on the universal permissions versus focusing on the restrictions. Toward the end of February, after months of home confinement, I flew to San Francisco and did a podcast interview with one of the leading marketing agencies in the health and well-being space about wellness, *Louisiana Catch*, and writing.

Why I spend 12 hours a week in Complete Silence

> "I've begun to realize that you can listen to silence and learn from it."
>
> —Chaim Potok, *The Chosen*

Do you remember the last time you sat intentionally in silence unless you were unwell or upset?

Once a week, for 12 hours straight, I turn my phone off along with my outside voice. My Dad gets nervous. "What if someone needs to reach you?" I joke that I am not an emergency room surgeon, so I can afford to disconnect and disengage. In those 12 hours, I don't speak, don't check emails and social media, don't read, don't watch anything on television or the iPad, and don't eat or drink. The only thing I am allowed is water, and maybe some herbal tea. And I look forward to the tranquility every week. It's been part of my weekly self-care practice for a few years now.

This vow of silence, known as *maun vrat* in Sanskrit, wasn't an alien concept to me. I grew up in an Indian home and had heard this term used often in conversations. But I didn't really see anyone practice *maun vrat* aside from my nana (maternal grandfather). He ate his meals in complete silence, found pockets of quietude during his day, and used his words like they were finite and precious. My nana was calm and unfazed by others' opinion of him. His words never hurt others. He could be in a room, surrounded by people, yet not allow anyone to burst his protective bubble. At six feet plus, well-built, light-skinned, and an extremely handsome man of few words, my nana was also the only one I knew who had a daily yoga practice. My last memory of him—a day before he died—was that of him doing *Hanuman asana*.

Decades passed, and I started to study Ayurveda. In the first few months of the program, our teacher told us about the role and importance of doing *maun vrat*. That it was a part of our curriculum. The entire class freaked out. Asking New Yorkers to not swear while crossing the road or roll our eyes in the subway or chew on something while watching television—that was just cruel! Was this some voodoo practice? No words or food or beverage or social engagements or books or writing from one Friday night until Sunday evening? I thought I would probably die because unspoken words would build a cobweb inside my mouth and suffocate me.

My husband and a few friends, who knew about the *maun vrat* at school, joked that I wouldn't last. 36 hours of quiet would drive me insane. I believed them because I am... maybe was... known for my insatiable appetite for words.

The night before *maun vrat* started, I ran into a gregarious senior of mine from Ayurveda school. She shared something that changed my life forever. The first night of her *maun vrat*, on her way back home from school, a car almost ran her over. Because she wasn't allowed to speak, she couldn't react. No foul words. No middle finger in the air. No narration of what had transpired. She confessed that she had never felt more in control of her life. One incident didn't send her hormones and temper raging. Her mind and adrenals weren't driven up the wall. Sure, the incident was scary, but she was okay and that's what mattered. In silence, she found perspective.

When *maun vrat* started for my cohort in Ayurveda school, I walked in, holding my senior's story tight. I listened to every word that poured out of my teacher's mouth. I thought of my nana and his demeanor. That night after class, when a few of my classmates and I got inside the subway, everything felt different. Instead of cackling about what had transpired in class or complaining about our work week or shimmying to music, we sat as a community, holding each other up in silence. No books. No phones. No whispers. We rooted for each other as we embraced silence. When I reached my subway stop, I experienced centeredness like never before. I noticed I was way less tired compared to other Fridays when returning home from school.

Our Ayurveda teacher had asked us to follow a few specific procedures to maximize the effects of the *maun vrat*. It was humbling to wake up and watch the sunrise and bow my head with humility. I practiced gentle yoga but didn't take a picture for social media. There was no reliance on instant gratification or external validation; instead, I processed the moment intimately and marveled at the beauty of Mother Nature. I felt a deep connection to the world around me.

At the end of 36 hours, we took pictures of our faces—we had also taken pictures before starting the *maun vrat* as part of our before and after shots. I shared them on social media and people started to ask if I had done something different. Apparently, my face looked fresher, my skin was glowing, and there was brightness in my eyes. I had noticed the difference in my mind but hadn't paid attention to the body.

My husband remarked that something inside of me had shifted. I was still and aligned. He found the transformation so profound that he asked if he too could join me for *maun vrat* every week. We keep the vow of silence for 12 hours because it is a lot more easily manageable, given our demanding lives. But we stay honest and do the *maun vrat* during a weekend day.

How did 36 hours make so much of a difference?

When you don't talk for many hours, you allow your mind and body deep rest. It teaches you self-control in an over-expressive world. When you don't watch TV or read or check emails, you are lowering your state of stimulation. You don't react, so your adrenal glands relax. Remember, the constant flight-or-fight syndrome that can lead to massive exhaustion and burnout eventually?

The *maun vrat* allows the parasympathetic system to become dominant, and as part of that, our muscles relax. Being relaxed makes us aware of our behavior. When we chat incessantly, we aren't mindful of what goes inside our body—both thoughts and food. By observing *maun vrat*, you start to pay attention to all the mindless emotional eating. You acknowledge the triggers. You eat when you are hungry, not when cortisol creates a false sense of hunger. The not-eating part allows the digestive system to take a break for a change. Every time that we put food or beverage in our mouth, our organs are put to work. If we need rest, why wouldn't our internal organs?

Honestly, in the beginning, keeping my mind quiet was a real struggle. I kept trying to shut up the inside voice. Staying away from technology, meditating, listening to my inner voice, and living in alignment with my thoughts didn't come overnight. Silence can be so loud! That dark space is where all our fears and insecurities and anxiety and creative blocks reside. *Maun vrat* meant I faced them head-on.

Slowly, I accepted that when we constantly talk and communicate, we abdicate our true strengths and struggles. We deny our inner voice what it deserves. The practice of yoga and meditation helped with my transformation tremendously. The combination reiterates the art of persistence and acceptance and living in the moment. They also help release stress. So much of our anxiety comes from worrying about tomorrow instead on focusing on today, and so we create a vicious cycle of stress.

Keeping this vow of silence has been extremely good for my writing, relationships, and overall wellness. When the thoughts arise, I observe and do not judge them, so there is a lot of peace within. I feel less angry and out of control when things go awry. I don't assume everything is being done to me, i.e. it's not personal. I know when I need to leave a conversation or room or relationship without being dramatic about it. I also believe that *maun vrat* has brought me closer to my own self. Self-care has become integral to who I am. Instead of fearing the million thoughts in my head or feeling alone in my own company, I have befriended them. I can actually sit with a blank mind on some days. I treat me-time as a sheer gift. Because I show myself compassion, I am authentic in my compassion toward others.

It's amazing how well I sleep when I keep *maun vrat*. Every cell and organ and emotion that makes me has had the chance to do detox and rejuvenate. When I approach my writing the next day, it comes from a reflective and focused space.

What Not to Say to Someone Living with Chronic Illness

"I often wished that more people understood the invisible side of things. Even the people who seemed to understand didn't, really."

—Jennifer Starzec, *Determination*

According to the Centers for Disease Control and Prevention, 6 out of 10 adults in the United States have a chronic illness. Chronic diseases are ongoing, generally incurable illnesses or conditions, such as heart disease, asthma, cancer, diabetes, and many more. Science tells us that these diseases are often preventable, and frequently manageable through early detection, improved diet, exercise, and treatment therapy.

The challenge for me comes from the illness being invisible. I appear to be physically okay but might be dealing with excruciating amounts of pain or low energy. I have had people say to me, "You look good. Why can't you party until late?" When someone said, "You do so much yoga, how could you fall sick?" I wanted to turn around and say, "I didn't choose to be sick. It wasn't my choice." But I have learned that my sanity and energy are important to me. It's not worth engaging in insipid conversations.

Part of my self-care regime is, no phone calls in the evening unless it's an emergency. I am at my job during the day and then work with clients, which leads to a heightened state of both energy and stress for extended periods of time. After my workouts and cooking dinner, I create space for myself. In the evenings, once we are done with dinner, I like to give my mind-body time to rest and recover, which means intentionally disconnecting. My condition flares up from stress, so I avoid any triggers. Prevention is better than any cure.

I often get asked, "You are still not speaking on the phone late in the evening?" like I'm starving a five-year old. It's infuriating when someone finds that my self-care seems radical and selfish when I don't impose my choices on them. If you haven't had to fight for your life in the emergency room of a hospital (Thank God!), you will never understand my stance. As Joseph Conrad once said, "The question is not how to get cured, but how to live."

Business owner Anne McAuley Lopez has chronic myeloid leukemia. She was diagnosed in July 2016, just four months after getting married. Here is what she'd like people to stop saying to cancer patients:

"You don't look like you have cancer."

"Wow. You've got your hair."

"Undetectable? That's remission. Congrats!" (NOTE: It is NOT remission. There is no remission for what I have. Undetectable is the best news we can get, so I let people be happy. It's easier than explaining all the time.)

"Your pain can't be that bad. You're out with us!"

Pragati Adhikari, an associate editor of a Hindi women's blog and a therapeutic artist and counselor who uses art for self-healing, has polycystic kidney disease. This disease took away much from her life. Apart from the physical, mental, and emotional stress, it gave Pragati a lot of anxiety and uncertainty. "But it's easier for you because you are used to sickness, surgeries and procedures," some said to her. She observed, "Things would come up when we are having discussions, like me wanting to rest (I don't have a fever so why would I be resting, right?), or when I say that now I feel more anxious on my visit to the hospital or just before a blood test or IVs (there is no long enough interval to forget the pain from the needle piercing you). The attitude is literally like, *I am used to living life with a sickness, so I should not complain about being tired or pushing myself all the time, because everyone is doing so much, everyone gets tired—so what is so special about me? Why should I be getting any special treatment? Because my parameters are normal, it's all in my mind now.*"

Mita Mistry, a columnist, mindfulness-based cognitive therapist, and acupuncturist, has Celiac disease. It is a chronic intestinal autoimmune condition. Her advice: "Avoid dismissing or minimizing someone's symptoms whether they are physical or mental health related. Comments like 'it could be worse' are really unhelpful and turn it into a competition for who feels the worst."

Ritu Saheb, Founder/Principal Architect at Saheb Architecture, also has Celiac disease, arthritis, and adrenal fatigue. "My illness is very manageable, and I have made huge strides. The most debilitating thing about it was exhaustion. People don't recognize that exhaustion is a real thing, and that a night's rest won't fix it. Or that food could flare up a chronic condition (as in my case). Especially because I am super-energetic and a high-achiever." Saheb has had servers in food service say to her, "Our food uses low-gluten wheat, or our bread is non-GMO, or gluten gets burnt off in our high-temperature pizza baking, or people who are gluten-free haven't had problems with our clam chowder." They simply don't know that if you have Celiac disease, gluten is literally poison to your body.

Living in Toronto and working as an account manager for an insurance brokerage, Nicola Blackwood has a condition called MdDS, which stands for Mal de Debarquement Syndrome. "It feels like you're constantly in motion even though physically you're not. The only sort of feeling of normalcy comes when you are actually mobile, as in traveling in a vehicle or train. Along with this illness comes severe anxiety," says Nicola. Looking at her, you wouldn't be able to tell. "But I take meds for anxiety just to keep a normal heart rate. People tell me *it's all in your head,* or *you're a hypochondriac.* Yup… but I let it slide. I'm tired of explaining."

I am not accusing everyone who says something insensitive to someone living with a chronic illness as being mean or intentionally cruel. But I have observed that many people walk into a room with assumptions and preconceived notions about another's situation. Instead of assuming how a friend or a family living with chronic illness is feeling, just ask without being presumptuous. And know that on some days, silence may be the best support.

WRITER'S CORNER

"If writing didn't require thinking then we'd all be doing it."
—Jeremiah Laabs

Writers are the case study for this section. But the sensibilities can be applied to any profession be it art, music, photography, accountancy, law, plumbing etc. We all have bills to pay and wellbeing to tend to.

Writers: Keep Your Heart Healthy and Your Stories Strong

Even though writing is one of the oldest and most enriching professions in the world, the writing lifestyle isn't all glamour. It brings along with it some health challenges. Writing (be it business or creative writing) is a stressful job that requires long hours of working in isolation and sitting in one place, often in bad posture. Over-stimulation of the nervous system using caffeine and alcohol is common amongst writers. The uncertainty and instability of the writing life may lead to sleep deprivation. As you can imagine, all of the above impacts heart health.

Heart disease is the number one killer of both men and women in America. Heart: it's where we writers lock up our stories, our insecurities, our inner conflicts, our darkness, our fears, and our loneliness. Heart: home to excessive emotional stress.

According to Ayurveda, the heart is the seat of a person's soul. A healthy heart is a natural reflection of our state of balance.

Here is what you can do to keep your heart and stories healthy:

Eat heart-healthy foods

When on a writing deadline, the last thing many writers focus is on what goes inside their bellies. Cans. Frozen meals. Instant noodles. Greasy takeout. And other forms of convenient, fast, junk foods become best friends with a writer on a deadline. Stop. End your relationship with excessiveness, be it alcohol or caffeine or late nights or smoking or refined sugars. Enjoy things in moderation. Reduce processed or canned foods, which can contribute to weight gain and toxic buildup. Drink at least 8-10 glasses of water. Hydration is important to help prevent clogging of the arteries. Buy organic or locally grown foods at the farmer's market whenever possible. Cook simple, one-dish meals. Food rich in Omega 3 fatty acids may reduce the risk of heart disease.

Don't forget to breathe

For a heart-healthy day, don't forget to breathe. How often have you caught yourself sighing, "Gosh, I didn't realize I have been at my laptop for the past X number of hours! Become aware. Remain mindful that breaks are important. Breathe deeply with intention. Specific pranayama or yogic breathing techniques calm the system. Many people can learn to reduce their blood pressure simply through breathing exercises. Look up alternate nostril breathing and thank yourself later.

Practice yoga asanas

A review of yoga and cardiovascular disease published in the *European Journal of Preventive Cardiology* indicates that yoga may help lower heart disease risk as much as conventional exercise, such as brisk walking. Yoga can also improve flexibility, muscle strength, and balance. Regular yoga practice may reduce levels of body-wide inflammation that contribute to the progression of heart disease. It may even lead to healthier blood pressure, cholesterol levels, blood sugar levels, and body weight—all factors that help reduce the risk of heart disease.

Quieten your mind

Meditation is integral to our mental well-being and promotes a healthy lifestyle. It impacts how you manage stress, and that affects your heart health. Writers who meditate often have more focus, clarity, and a deeper connection to their inner self and stories. They are more capable of separating good stuff from the chaos. Meditation can create happiness. That happiness comes from self-acceptance. It helps you handle rejections and bad reviews with a healthier perspective. It calms the nervous system and lowers both anxiety and stress. According to Dan Harris, author of *Ten Percent Happier*, "Science experiments have found that people who practice meditation release significantly lower doses of cortisol, known as the stress hormone. This is consequential because frequent release of cortisol can lead to heart disease, diabetes, dementia, cancer, and depression."

Set healthier boundaries.

It's important to protect your energy. Doing so protects your stories and heart. It's absolutely fine to cancel a commitment. It's OK to say a NO to phone calls or a dinner invite. Say NO to what doesn't nourish you. Don't forget to include "me-time" on your schedule. I am not suggesting you turn into a recluse but be mindful of who and what you allow into your life. As writers, especially when we are in the middle of the creative process, our skin becomes thin. Through osmosis, we absorb every word and criticism. Sensitivity and emotions become our guides, but they can also leave us feeling vulnerable.

Get moving

Writing requires sitting in one place for extended periods of time, which can be terrible for your posture, back, neck, and weight gain. Studies have found just 60 to 90 minutes a week of physical activity can reduce your heart disease risk by up to 50 percent. The workout doesn't have to be elaborate or fancy—take the stairs, go for a walk, take a dance class—just get moving.

Joanna Elm once said, "There is no better job in the whole world than being a writer." I concur from the bottom of my heart!

Writers, Let's Talk About the F-Word: Finances

When you come face-to-face with death, fears leave you. You know your time is up, and you stop fighting. There is a feeling on the inside, which is more real than anything else, and that is about acceptance and surrendering. No matter how many TV shows and movies make fun of cleaning up your browser history before they unplug you, that's not what plagues your mind when you think it's your end. Or maybe it's just me.

I remember seeing my husband's face, and my doctor cousin emphatically explaining something to other nurses and doctors. I recall the beautiful view of the world outside from my hospital room as my own world turned inside out with strange faces hovering over and prodding me. You know who and what broke my self-pity reverie? Another hospital staff member. She was polite, courteous, and diligent. She turned to my husband amidst all the chaos and spoke softly, "Would you like to pay the bill in full, or we can talk about monthly installments?"

I have never felt worse in my life. I was going to die and leave behind a medical debt for my husband?! Imagine… if that's the last thought that nudges you when you believe you have a few breaths left.

A few hours later, I opened my eyes and saw my husband and cousin smile at me. The medicines and prayers and my resilience had worked. But in that instance, I knew something had to change. Money—something I never really thought of before—had surfaced on my list of priorities. The transformation came from realizing that for someone who wrote about women's empowerment and worked with rape and domestic violence survivors and spent 90% of her workday making other people's lives better through coaching and speaking engagements, I hadn't planned my own finances very well.

My story didn't end at the ER or the hospital room that week of September 2018. Once I was discharged from the hospital, I remained homebound unless you count trips to several specialists, ultrasound scans, MRIs, and the surgeon's office. I couldn't eat, sleep, write, read, or walk. Between losing 35–40 lbs. within 10 weeks to losing my clients because I didn't know if and when I would get better, I didn't recognize my life. On a weekly basis, I had 4–5 doctor appointments. Between doctor visits and their co-pays, Uber charges, and medicines, the medical bills added up over the 5–6 months.

I promised myself that if I managed to fight my illness and stay alive, I would do anything to rebuild my body and life, starting with finding financial stability. I wouldn't stop writing or consider closing my business. But I would find stable, bi-weekly paychecks.

I have worked for over 20 years now. But, as a writer, creative entrepreneur, and small business owner, I hadn't planned for short-term disability. Sickness is impartial and humbling. It can get to anyone, especially when you least expect it. These are the facts, as I see them:

- **Writing doesn't always pay very well**—This is a known fact. And on those occasions when it does (if you get a large signing amount as advance for your book), the earnings might not still be enough to sustain yourself after paying your agent, taxes, book promotion and tour expenses, new clothes, photographer etc. It's easy to romanticize frugal living and minimize your materialistic needs. But medical emergencies, like mine, are real. Deaths and losses are real. Chances are, as we get older, the body will need more attention and maintenance. That requires money!

- **A financially dependable partner**—Writers tend to be touchy about this topic but many writers I know are able to write full-time because: (1) they have a partner who is the breadwinner, and (2) they come from a family with money. That is great until the arrangement stops working. We have all known people who lost their jobs. What happens when the breadwinning partner is out of a job, even if temporarily? Doesn't it feel selfish to pursue your writing dream while the other person is out finding options to provide for the family?

- **Relationships end**—In the last year alone, a few of my writer friends and colleagues have found themselves in broken marriages and/or their relationships ended unexpectedly. Relationships are hard work (I say this despite being happily married). And being married to a writer isn't exactly easy. We live in our own worlds and create an alternate reality. Our egocentrism and unconventionality aren't easy for everyone to comprehend. When relationships end, responsibilities don't. Can you see how scrambling to look for a job and starting your life from scratch while sustaining a writing career isn't easy?

- **Financial stability is good for your mental health**—The writing life is rife with stress, insecurities, solitude, sleeplessness, anxiety, and other challenges. A lot of these issues stem from not knowing what might happen *tomorrow* and not having a dependable schedule or income stream. The intense motivation, the working in isolation, the vivid imagination, and the magical inspiration are so necessary for creativity and breakthroughs. But they can also be detrimental for your mental health, if that's all you do. Being accountable to a colleague or a boss can be empowering and help you prioritize better.

- **Writing imitates life**—If we are chained to our writing desks all day, not talking to many people, not assimilating in the "real world," not experiencing stories, where and how will we learn about life? Can you rely only on imagination to create a masterpiece?

- **Boost your confidence**—Having a well-paying job outside of writing can be great for your confidence and your relationship with writing. Writing is a big part of who I am and how I see the world. But meeting deadlines in the office and showing up for my clients are equally important aspects of my work life. It makes my relationship with writing that much more sacred and cherished. Not having the luxury to stare into space all day makes me more productive when I show up to my words. I have dedicated writing time. I write the stories truest to me, and not another article/essay because my next meal is dependent on the essay being sold, you know? I am also pickier with the clients I sign up as an Ayurveda-based mindset and wellness coach, because I have the financial and emotional stability from my paychecks.

- **Helps you hire the best**—If you are feeling stuck in your writing and want to work with an experienced coach or sign the best editor in town or hire a publicist for your book launch or go away to a secluded space to write or find a virtual assistant, all of it requires the F-word, finance.

For a writer, being financially sustainable should be just as sacred as creating time for your writing. I have been to writing residencies and author gatherings and attended online conversations (writing communities), where being broke as a writer is romanticized. Let's not delude ourselves and those entering the world of writing for even one moment that we can survive on love, fresh air, and inspiration.

I am not suggesting that every writer needs to get a 9-5 job or work for the corporate world. All I am saying is that we need to have honest conversations about the role and value of money in our daily lives—for ourselves, our families, and our future. Money is not a despicable word. Being bitter about it or living in denial isn't a luxury we creative professionals can afford any longer. While money won't buy you happiness, it does make life and writing easier. There is nothing despicable about a man or a woman who can provide for his or her family. It's selfish to believe that your writing is the only important thing in the world.

7 Wellness Tips for Writers That Will Impact on Their Writing

> "Take care of your body. It's the only place you have to live."

> —Jim Rohn

For the past six months, I have been going through different doors of hell when it comes to my health. But I am here, and today I am writing. Such is the power of the human mind and body.

One could argue, what's the point of living a healthy and balanced lifestyle if you are going to end up in the hospital fighting for your life? Fair enough. Here is my counterargument: I came back from the dead and my body is healing because I have made it a point to prioritize my physical and emotional health. I went from not being able to open the front door to our apartment to taking the subway last week. Even my family physician and the surgeon were shocked (in a good way) that I wasn't depressed despite everything I have been through. I always remind them that none of this is by chance. I attribute my journey of healing and recovery and staying mentally strong and re-establishing my relationship with creativity to the seven things included below.

Mindful food choices

How you eat is as important for your overall health as what you eat. It's easy to get distracted with a plethora of information and diet trends out there. And if you are a foodie like me, things get even more confusing. Should I eat gluten or avoid gluten? What about dairy and grains? Is Keto good? How is it different from Paleo? If you have a health issue, that's different; otherwise, listen to your body since it holds the ultimate wisdom. Pay attention to how your body reacts to foods. Pay attention to how certain foods make you feel emotionally. Revisit the food intelligence your grandma shared. We are all busy, I know, so keep it simple. But pay attention to what you put inside your body. For instance, avoid caffeine and alcohol close to bedtime as they can interfere with your sleep cycle. Avoid eating heavy and spicy meals late at night. Honor seasonal fruits and vegetables and include them in your diet.

Cultivate a daily meditation practice

Meditation is a writer's best friend. It can help reduce anxiety, improve concentration, calm the nerves, alleviate stress, protect your energy, offer perspective, create stronger focus, help better connect with your creativity, formulate newer ideas, and teach you about acceptance. Start simple with mindful breathing. The goal is to focus only on breathing and to ignore other thoughts that enter the mind. Breathe slowly and deeply, counting your breaths or otherwise focusing on your breaths. Even experienced meditators get a stream of intruding thoughts. The trick is to allow them and return to the chosen focus: breath.

Soothe away stress

Think about what happens to our body when we're stressed or anxious. It handicaps the immune system and increases the risk of diseases. The heart rate increases as our mind races. A combination of the above affects the quality of our thoughts. Stress activates areas of the brain that make us more alert. It also elevates production of hormones, including cortisol, that interfere with and disrupt normal sleep-wake cycles. One can reduce stress and anxiety through meditation, yoga, and sometimes, chamomile tea.

Think positively

Our mind is always occupied by thoughts and they influence our every action. Can you imagine how much we limit ourselves in every aspect of our lives if we give negative thoughts too much power? We don't write that book because we think our work is too unimportant and nobody would want it. We don't send in our essay or story or poem to any publications because we assume rejection in return. We don't live the life of our dreams because our negative thoughts have decided for us that we aren't worth it. We don't take care of our health because we believe we are too weak to push our limits and will never feel better. So, do you see how we become our thoughts?

This doesn't mean that we pretend all is well and there is sunshine everywhere. That would qualify for toxic positivity. It just means that we fight our inner demons—the ones that nudge us about our failures and fears and insecurities and end—with our true, positive thoughts.

For every negative thought that emerges, we respond to it with a positive thought without pretending all is okay. Say your gratitude for the good in your life. I promise, it makes the most arduous of days bearable.

Exercise with joy

Not everyone wants to run a marathon. Not everyone cares about doing a headstand or showing up to a Barre class or a CrossFit session. Good news: you don't have to. Find out what works for you. It could be walking or running with a buddy or climbing stairs or some other form of physical activity. But exercise with joy because it can help with your brain health and memory. Exercise can improve the quality of your sleep and energy levels. Overall, it can make you feel happier. Yes, as writers, we don't need to dwell in darkness and depression to be creative because that kind of mindset is both dangerous and unproductive.

Don't ignore sleep hygiene

There is a stereotype about writers and poets (maybe creative professionals overall) that we all need the silence of the dead-of-night to be at our creative best. Bouncing off the walls as we carry our sleep-deprived bodies through deadlines is romanticized. Not all of us are night owls. If anything, research shows that night owls might have to deal with health consequences of their lifestyle. Messing around with your sleep cycle can disrupt hormonal balance in the body and birth pessimistic thoughts.[2] An article, on sleep disorders, in WebMD tells us that night owls are nearly twice as likely as early risers to have a psychological disorder and 30 percent more likely to have diabetes. Their risk for respiratory disease was 23 percent higher and for gastrointestinal disease 22 percent higher.

Energize your body

As writers, we sit for extended periods of time—refilling cups of chai and coffee, looking out the window, talking to our characters, mulling over ideas, doing research on our laptops, and reading through piles of books. While the coziness of this arrangement might sound good, Mayo Clinic tells us that too much sitting overall and prolonged periods of sitting also seem to increase the risk of death

---

[2] https://www.webmd.com/sleep-disorders/news/20180412/who-lives-longer---night-owls-or-early-birds

from cardiovascular disease.[3] Get up from your seat. Do some stretches or neck and shoulder rotation, or just drink some water. Whatever it takes, move.

Nothing is more important than your health. If you nurture your mind and body, they nourish your creativity.

---

[3] https://www.mayoclinic.org/healthy-lifestyle/adult-health/expert-answers/sitting/faq-20058005

The Power of Positivity In Storytelling

"Our happiness depends on the habit of mind we cultivate."
Norman Vincent Peale, *The Power of Positive Thinking*

I have had several folks tell me that they constantly feel that the world is coming to an end. Between the pandemic, racism, environmental collapse, and world leaders losing their marbles, most of us are feeling traumatized. It doesn't help that so many are still working remotely with minimal social interaction, cued into the news constantly, and scrolling through social media where we end up watching/listening to a lot of negativity.

People are naturally attracted to negative news. Call it a way of promoting survival. Our brains are primed to scan the environment for danger and remember threats. But the constant focus on negativity leads to a stress response that goes on and on. That state is there to deal with a physical emergency. Because running away from a tiger takes a lot of energy, parts of our body not immediately needed are shut down. This includes digestion and the immune system.

When you start believing in that negativity, you don't pay attention to what you consume (food, media, and thoughts) because you start to think everything is pointless. I believe that there is still a lot of good in this world. I do believe there are many reliable people who can make positive change. It is unfortunate that our mainstream media often wants us to think the opposite. Honestly, it takes a shift in the mindset and an effort to see the good that's also there. Staying positive is the best defense against stress.

The idea that your mind can change your world almost seems too good to be true. But it works. Don't just focus on what's not working. I am not suggesting that we ignore the status quo. But my suggestion is to seek that ray of light that urges you to navigate the world through kindness and positivity. For all the negative stories we write and hear, can we make an intentional effort to share positive words as well? As Chimamanda Adichie said in her talk, *The Danger of a Single Story,* at TEDGlobal 2009, "Many stories matter. Stories have been used to dispossess and to malign. But stories can also be used to empower, and to humanize. Stories can break the dignity of a people. But stories can also repair that broken dignity."

It's important to see and share the truth. But the truth is that every culture has several stories. Don't adhere to just the ones about negativity. I hear some of my closest African American friends remind us that they want us to celebrate Black culture with joy. Don't read and watch material that only focuses on Black victimization; be curious and educate yourself about stories of empowerment as well. There are so many inspiring moments born from BLM protests.

Experiences of positive emotions are central to human nature and contribute richly to the quality of people's lives. In Bollywood and media in India, we mostly hear/read stories about patriarchy, violence against women, and gender inequality. Yes, these are all truths that must be told. But India has also produced powerful female role models like Indira Gandhi (Former Prime Minister), Shakuntala Devi (Known as the "human calculator," she is in the Guinness Book of World Records), Indra Nooyi (Former CEO, Pepsico), and Priyank Chopra Jonas (Former Miss World and star of hit show *Quantico*). Can we talk about them as well to inspire?

In *Constructive Journalism: The Effects of Positive Emotions and Solution Information in News Stories,* Karen McIntyre[4] tells us that people who read inspiring news stories are more willing afterward to sign up for generous actions related to the story, such as signing a petition or donating money to support a cause from the story.

Stories are a powerful tool for learning. I believe that positive, empowering stories can have huge educational value. It takes gumption to make intentional efforts to stay on the side of positivity and tell positive stories. But including daily doses of positivity—a cultivated habit—can change how we see the world. It is actually good for our mental health as well as relationships.

[4] https://cdr.lib.unc.edu/concern/dissertations/rn3012085

How Calming the Mind Can Help a Writer

At the 2014 Academy Awards, Robert De Niro's intro of the best screenplay nominees caught the attention of many. "The mind of a writer can be a truly terrifying thing," he said, before continuing, "Isolated, neurotic, caffeine-addled, crippled by procrastination and consumed by feelings of panic, self-loathing, and soul-crushing inadequacy. And that's on a good day." His comment was cruelly funny and spot-on.

Writers face a greater risk of depression, anxiety disorders, and substance abuse. The stresses of the writing life—constant rejections, uncertainty, erratic highs and lows, and usually low pay may add fuel to the fire of insecurity. But, over the years, I've come to learn that there are ways in which a writer's mind can remain calm and healthy: that magic word is meditation. I am not guaranteeing that meditation is what will turn you into an international, award-winning, best-selling, prolific writer. But with daily meditation practice, you start owning your writing, stop leaving things to chance and moods and whims, and put an end to the self-victimization when rejections come your way.

Why meditation?

Meditation can help you tap into your full creative juices and allow you to unravel the layers of ideas trapped deep inside your mind. Between social media, emails, newsletters, online ads, we are constantly bombarded with hot writing trends and best-selling genres. In this overstimulated state, the pressure to blindly follow what others are doing can be high. Meditation calms your nerves and allows the brain to process the information it has soaked up from over-engaging. Meditation also trains the mind to turn off the outside stimuli and focus on the inside. That's when you can connect with the ideas within and make honest discoveries about what you want to write about, not what others think you should write about.

Imaging at the Osher Research Center found that people who practiced mindful meditation were able to adjust the brain wave that screens out distractions and increase their productivity more quickly that those who did not meditate. [5]

Ever felt stuck in your writing? Or do you have any manuscripts catching dust? Or do you find yourself ineffectively juggling multiple projects and then judging yourself harshly for not succeeding? Meditation changes both the function and structure of the brain to support self-control. It can help improve focus and attention; as a result, it can reduce fatigue. It reduces stress levels and alleviates anxiety. If we can reduce stress, our creativity and ideas have the space to become more lucid.

Meditation can help protect your energy. Cultivating a daily meditation practice can lower the effects of the emotionally crippling disease I've referred to previously, called FOMO (fear of missing out) where we overextend ourselves and feel the need to be present at all the readings and events. Meditation teaches you be present in the moment and show up for people and events that mean something to you. And not mindlessly say a YES to the million invites that are darted your way just because you fear you'll miss out. It's important to prioritize your writing days and creative energy. A calm and focused mind, a gift of meditation, will help formulate newer ideas.

You don't have to tell me, but have you ever been jealous of a fellow writer beyond reasonable understanding? Have you felt insecure over an extended period of time about your writing career and done things (even if unintentionally) to sabotage your health and sanity? Well, meditation improves a wide range of willpower skills, including impulse control. It encourages a healthy lifestyle and makes you more compassionate. Once you become kinder to yourself and understand that someone else's success isn't a reflection on your failures, you will automatically become more compassionate toward others.

Meditation teaches us self-acceptance. Not everyone becomes a Pulitzer Prize winner or wins a grant, and that is okay. Find out why you write what you write and carve out your very own path to creative happiness.

Meditation gives you the courage to speak up, as it also increases self-awareness. That said, sometimes, speaking up and speaking out

---

[5]   https://www.oshercollaborative.org/video/your-brain-meditation-how-meditation-impacts-brain-and-implications-health

can create for a lonely existence. And "feeling alone" can impact your emotional and physical health negatively.

If a few years ago you'd told me that I would rely on a daily meditation practice to elevate my creativity and productivity, I would have rolled my eyes. This is because, like many others, I used to believe that writers and artists thrive best under chaos. I used to think bouncing off the walls and sleepless minds contribute to the making of a successful writer/poet/artist. I am grateful to have been proven wrong. Meditation is a gift, which is simple, easy, and rewarding. Embrace it so you don't rob yourself of the opportunity to become the best writer you can be on so many levels.

I invite you to take out 10 minutes every day. Set an alarm, so the monkey-brain doesn't keep nagging, "Are we done yet?" Close your eyes and focus on your breath. You can sit or lie down. Thoughts will arise. Don't judge them. Don't question any feelings. Just observe. Every time that your mind wanders, bring it back to the breath. Or, try the body scan meditation. This allows practitioners to scan areas of tension. You start at one end of the body, usually the feet, and work your way up. The goal is to notice tension and to allow it to release.

How What You Eat Impacts Your Mood and Creativity

What we eat impacts our mood. But this is more important for people engaged in creative activities like writing, because writing is an emotional job that tells us that some level of emotional instability accompanies the profession. Think about writers and creativity. We, the writers, create from a place of vulnerability. As the wise say, "There is no great genius without some touch of madness."[6]

A study in the *Indian Journal of Psychiatry*, "Creativity and mental health: A profile of writers and musicians" by K.S. Pavitra, C.R. Chandrashekhar, and Partha Choudhury, suggests an increased rate of schizophrenia, manic-depressive disorder, depression, personality disorder, or alcoholism in creative individuals. For some, the causation can be the other way—suffering makes people good at creativity. A rejection or a cruel note from an editor or a heart-wrenching review or a debilitating writer's block—in what direction do you find yourself headed?

Be honest; don't you find your feet dragging you to the pantry-kitchen-dining area of your home? How often do we eat our emotions in the form of sugar or drink it in some form of alcoholic beverage or drown our feelings in cups of caffeine? And, how often do you wake up the next day feeling like someone destroyed your mind-body with all the foods, caffeine, and alcohol you ingested? And then starts the deep-rooted relationship with lethargy, procrastination, creative block, and self-loathing, no?

So, what is the connection between your diet, moods, and creativity? For starters, there is a close relationship between your brain and gut. There is a reason that the gastrointestinal tract is referred to as your "second brain."[7]

Your GI tract is home to billions of bacteria. These bacteria influence the production of neurotransmitters like serotonin that constantly carry messages from the gut to the brain. What does serotonin do? It helps mediate mood and social behavior, appetite and digestion, sleep, memory, and inhibits pain. About 90–95% of

---

[6] https://www.ncbi.nlm.nih.gov/pmc/articles/PMC2899997/
[7] https://my.clevelandclinic.org/health/treatments/16358-gut-brain-connection

serotonin is produced in your digestive tract. Doesn't it make sense that the digestive system doesn't just help you digest food, but also guides your emotions? Do you see the correlation between what you eat and its direct impact on creativity and productivity?

Eating healthy food promotes the growth of "good" bacteria, which in turn positively affects serotonin production. Good bacteria lower inflammation and positively impact nutrient absorption. A steady consumption of sugar, alcohol, too much caffeine, and junk food, on the other hand, can cause inflammation that hampers production of serotonin. When neurotransmitter production is optimal, your brain receives positive messages loud and clear. And you see your emotions reflect it. But when serotonin production goes awry, so might your mood. Do writers need to be reminded about our emotions and moods and how that can impact our writing days?

A few experts have been specifically examining the relationship between gut health and creativity. Research tells us that sugar, in particular, is considered a major culprit of inflammation, and it feeds the "bad" bacteria in the GI tract. Certain studies have tied sugar to mental decline and foods that are rich in vitamins and minerals, e.g. freshly squeezed green juice to promote well-being, curiosity, and creativity. Vitamin C is an essential factor in the production of dopamine, which is the neurotransmitter that underlies motivation and promotes engagement. A report published in the *British Journal of Health Psychology* studied about 400 young adults over 13 days and found that eating more fruits and vegetables correlates to better well-being and an increased sense of curiosity and creativity.[8]

Eating well has many lifelong benefits. Start paying attention to how eating different foods make you feel—not just in the moment, but even the next day. It may be days or weeks before you start to feel the mood-boosting and overall positive effects of a better diet. But it will happen. The mind and body will respond positively. Eating healthy will motivate you to exercise regularly and take better care of yourself overall. When we feel good about ourselves and feel physically and emotionally stronger, it directly impacts our creativity and productivity. When you stick to a diet of healthy food, you're setting yourself up for fewer mood fluctuations and an improved ability to focus. Isn't that something all of us writers can appreciate—

---

[8] https://pubmed.ncbi.nlm.nih.gov/25080035/

feeling positive, being creative, and experiencing fewer emotional upswings?

Writers: Empower Yourself with Self-Care

We, the writers, careful observers of human nature and society, retreat back to isolation to create. Sure, we rely on a supportive community—online and offline—that holds us in our weaknesses and strengths as we interpret the world for others. Chai and coffee brew along with our stories. But creativity is mostly a solo process. A quiet room, a stained cup, piles of paper, glasses, manuscripts gathering dust, rejection letters, and the buds of new ideas. Yes, while the solitude seems like rocket fuel for our creativity, the isolation may not always be the best option for our wellness.

Why self-care matters on a whole different and deeper level for writers and artists

Writing about emotional experiences may improve mental health eventually. But writing hurts before it heals. And there are times when with our words—using the vessel of poetry, fiction, or nonfiction—we create an alternate reality. Sometimes, the alternate reality is prettier than our real lives.

Existing between the lines of realism and creativity can be hard. Geniuses like Sylvia Plath, Hunter Thomson, Virginia Woolf, Ernest Hemingway, Yukio Mishima, Anne Sexton, and David Foster Wallace told us stories about the world; but when it came to their own lives, they found it hard to cope with reality. Researchers have found writers to have more than double the risk of schizophrenia and bipolar disorder compared to a control group of accountants[9]. Writers also face a greater risk of depression, anxiety disorders, and substance abuse.

There are also the stresses of the writing life — constant rejections, uncertainty, and usually low pay add fuel to the fire of insecurity.

Dear writers: Make time for YOU and actually care for yourself. When we hear self-care, a lot of us assume that it means spending big money at a spa. Many of us believe that self-care is self-seeking. The old Vedic texts remind us that self-care matters and it isn't selfish. No

---

[9] https://electricliterature.com/the-writing-life-writing-and-mental-health/

one can serve and heal others from an empty pot. Like it or not, writers often come up "empty" because writing is an emotional job.

Self-care can be simple. Start with your emotional health. What is that you *need*? In my novel, *Louisiana Catch*, the female protagonist Ahana—a 33-year-old grieving daughter and sexual abuse survivor from New Delhi—must summon the courage to run a feminist conference in New Orleans, trust a man she meets over the Internet, and unravel the mystery of an online predator in order to find her power. Pausing, reflecting, caring for herself (by befriending silence, going for a run, and practicing yoga), spending time with those who uplift her are a few of her chosen self-care methods. What will be yours?

How Mindfulness Can Help You Enjoy Your Book Release Day

> "On the road to success, there is always room to share appreciation and gratitude for other people's successes. Feeling gratitude for other people raises our own vibration, while adding cement to the bricks we lay."
>
> —Alaric Hutchinson, *Living Peace*

It's 5 am on Saturday, April 7, 2018. My head is ready to explode. I am supposed to speak at a wellness conference in Pennsylvania in a few hours, and on Tuesday, April 10, my debut U.S. novel, *Louisiana Catch,* comes out. That very evening, I am doing an intimate wine and reading celebration with a fellow author at the Bluestockings bookstore in downtown Manhattan.

Louisiana Catch is my 12th book. It wasn't an easy book to write, because the female protagonist is a sexual assault survivor. I teach yoga to survivors of sexual assault, rape, and domestic violence. All of it feels too personal. Though the book's release happens to coincide with the #MeToo movement, and the media attention has been heart-warming, none of it has been a cake walk.

To an outsider, this is all good stress, right? What you dreamed about. What you worked toward. You know within that the creative life is a gift, but it is also full of ups and downs. It is exhilarating and nerve-wracking in the same breath. Of course, then there are elements outside of our control. How will our book be welcomed into the world? Will anyone read it? What if no one shows up to the book launch events? The list of anxiety triggers can be endless.

To stay stable and productive, I have followed a few tips and tricks that have helped me stay focused in this journey. I am no expert, but I hope a few of these suggestions will help and make your big day one to remember.

Be kind

Having a book coming out doesn't give you the license to be a jerk. Yes, you have a lot on your mind during this time. So many of these emotions you can't explain in words because a writer's mind is layered and complex. Talk to those you trust—close friends and family—and let them know that your emotions might be extreme on some days. Allow yourself some space and room for failure. Rest. Recuperate. When you are kind to yourself, you will automatically be kind to others.

Don't let success get to your head

We are only as good as our last book. I cannot even list the number of rejections I have had and will continue to have—that's part of being a writer. In the same breath, I have also won awards and my books have gone on to become bestsellers. What's kept me grounded is knowing that success is just as fleeting as failure. The only constant is change. Don't let your literary performance affect the core of who you are and how you conduct yourself in the world.

Build relationships

The world can feel like a lonely place if you alienate everyone. Know what matters to you. Writing is one of the most important reasons for my life, but it isn't the only one. Spending time with my family and friends is what sustains me. Sharing a meal with them or going away on trips or sipping wine together or listening to their stories or showing up to the yoga studio, it keeps my life and creativity in perspective. I am not saying that's the only way to build relationships. But… it's important to have a few people in your life who are there for you, regardless of your external successes and failures.

Practice appreciation

Remember, you have a book deal, which means someone believes in your work. That in itself is pretty darn amazing! You managed to finish writing an entire book. Did someone have your back during this process? Don't forget to say thanks for all that you have. Don't forget to say gratitude for what you don't have. Every experience helps us grow. Every person we meet has something to teach us. When gratitude becomes a part of your practice, you will notice the difference in your happiness quotient.

Pay it forward.

Take a breath and make a mental note of those who have helped you along the way. Right from my husband, who made space in our lives so I could write *Louisiana Catch,* to organizations like Lululemon and Exhale To Inhale that have come together to help me host my April 18th book launch event in NYC... I couldn't have done it all by myself. I made a vow that I will support other writers, so at all of my *Louisiana Catch* readings across the United States, I have invited other authors or yoga professionals or publishers or creative writing instructors to come and share the space with me and share their books and stories. For instance, on April 18, at the Lululemon Hub Seventeen, we had a panel discussion between a psychotherapist, yoga teacher, meditation teacher, and me. I believe that the more of us come together to share our work, the more we understand the need for stories.

5 Yoga Poses Beneficial for Writers and Artists

Disclaimer: This content is purely informative and educational in nature and should not be construed as medical advice. Please use the content only in consultation with an appropriately certified and experienced yoga teacher.

Let's be honest. Whatever the medium of your creative expression, you probably struggle with few or all of these: shutting down your mind, dealing with a stiff neck and shoulders, chattering of the monkey mind, getting affected by the ups and downs of the creative process, battling achy wrists, and fighting insomnia. Just think about it... if our mind, body, and spirit are cluttered with thoughts and distress, how can we create? After all, creativity does arise best in moments of stillness.

Here's the truth. The creative process can be a little hard on the body—both physically and emotionally. Be it the long-standing hours on the feet for an artist, hours spent typing on a computer for a writer/poet or battling artistic blocks or the emotional havoc creativity can unleash, you know the damage it can do. When the physical body suffers, so does the creative process.

Why creativity needs mindfulness

When I was on a deadline for my novel, *Louisiana Catch*, there came a time when I just wanted to be with my characters in the alternate reality that I had created, not the intruding world. I sat in one place for hours at a stretch. I went to bed thinking about my characters and wanted to spend every waking hour deciphering their next move. The only thing on my mind at every given point—my book.

Despite being a yoga teacher and "knowing" about it all, I let go of the mindfulness during my creative process. This wreaked havoc on my mind and body. My digestion and sleep felt a little off. The compressed chest, contracted spine, knotted thighs, and tight hips became a roadblock in the path of my creativity and productivity. I was constantly exhausted and emotional. I had to return to my daily yoga practice.

How yoga heals the body and mind

Yoga is renowned for stimulating the parasympathetic nervous system, calming you down, and restoring overall balance in your life. It holds special qualities that can help creative professionals. Yes, it can free up tight hips, loosen tight muscles, elongate a compressed spine, and bring relief to our achy back and neck. But yoga does more than that. It trains us to endure as well as enjoy the demands of the artistic process, be it by relieving us from the creative block, alleviating body pain, pursuing new inspirational paths, lowering physical and emotional tension, or reducing doubts around creativity.

Yoga is moving meditation. Connecting the mind, body, and spirit and integrating it with your creative journey can liberate your authentic voice while nurturing your physical body. Yoga can help lower the amount of cortisol in your brain. This hormone activates the amygdala, also known as the fear center in the brain, and shrinks the pre-frontal cortex, which manages self-control and discipline.

Yoga asanas for creative professionals

- **Head-To-Knee Forward Bend** (*Janusirsasana*) This pose improves digestion and relieves any anxiety or fear. It stretches the spine, shoulders, hamstrings, and groins. It also calms the brain and helps relieve mild depression.

- **Supported Shoulder Stand** (*Salamba Sarvangasana*) This pose opens the throat chakra, which governs self-expression and our ability to communicate effectively. It also benefits the shoulders and neck and stimulates the thyroid gland.

- **Bridge Pose** (*Setu Bandhasana*) This pose calms the brain and central nervous system. It also improves the circulation of blood and stretches the chest, neck, spine, and hips. This pose strengthens the back, buttocks, and hamstrings.

- **Tree Pose** (*Vrksasana*) This pose is known to enhance confidence and create a more positive level of self-esteem. Standing tall and proud with good posture, whether in a variation or balancing wholeheartedly on one foot, the alignment alone broadens the shoulders, opens your heart, and raises your feel-good factor.

- **Legs-Up-The-Wall Pose** (*Viparita Karani*) This pose relieves tired or cramped legs and feet. It gently stretches the back legs, front torso, and the back of the neck. It also calms the mind and relieves mild backaches.

Just know that adopting a routine yoga practice benefits not only your physical health but also your emotional, spiritual, and psychological well-being. You get more dopamine and serotonin by doing yoga—these chemicals help you feel more relaxed and readier to handle whatever stressful situation is thrown at you.

Why Working Out Is Imperative for Writers and Their Writing

When we talk about writers and the creative life, we rarely talk about their wellness. If anything, brokenness, misery, pain, and being poor are often spotlighted. We associate tea, coffee, whisky, and wine with writing, which is all fun! But I wish we had more proactive conversations around writers' well-being. I want to see more panels at literary conferences on the impact of working out on creativity because the correlation cannot be ignored. Physical activity is good for your brain, which means it's good for your writing.

For those on the outside, writing appears to be a glamorous profession. I have readers, friends, and family ask if the royalty from my 12 books will work toward my retirement plan. I chuckle on the inside and go about my day job and consulting business. So many see authors at author events and pictures of literary celebrations and assume that's the essence of the writing life—people, wine, photos, chic outfits, and glamour.

Being a writer is a gift indeed. But it's not the easiest life. The reality is that writing is a sedentary activity and a solitary profession. Writers spend the majority of their workday hunched over a laptop or tucked away in front of a notebook while living inside their heads. Sometimes they are clad in pajamas and perched on their couch; other times, they're trying to turn invisible at crowded coffee shops. Not every city in the world has dedicated coworking spaces for writers. Fingers tapping the keyboard harshly, pen scribbling in pages, steam from tea/coffee creating a mystical fog, eyebrows furrowing in concentration, hands running over the chin in frustration as well as contemplation. Paralyzed by fears and insecurities, battling anxiety and depression, ruminating over the mystery of human behavior, wondering if they will make enough to pay the rent, contemplating inexpensive eating options, and reliving traumas and uncomfortable scenarios. Well, you get the picture!

There is not much standing up or moving around or stretching of the body happening through the writing process. And, once the writing deadline gets closer, the majority of writers ignore the need for social interaction, the body's need to move, and good night's sleep. They isolate themselves and live inside their cocoons. None of these choices are good for their health or writing.

Writers can notoriously abstain from exercise. Sitting all day, every day, is dangerous. It can impact your posture as well as creative abilities. The less you sleep, the less chance your body and brain have to heal. There is no arguing that this lifestyle isn't the best choice to battle writer's block either.

Ever noticed that, depending on how productive or unproductive your writing day has been, your mood wavers? Ever feel low and lonely at the end of a writing day? Working out can give you fresh perspective on your writing.

Unplug and move. Step away from the distractions of emails, social media, conference calls, grocery lists, household chores, family obligations, and other social commitments. Movement is good for recharging and refreshing our mental pathways. It will bring you creative freedom. I have come up with new creative ideas for projects, character development techniques, dialogues, book titles, promotional partnerships, book endings, essay ideas, marketing, and publicity strategies while working out. How you move is your choice: walking, dancing, running, yoga, high-intensity interval training, tai chi, swimming. But do include a good workout in your writing routine because exercise increases blood flow and oxygen levels in the brain.

Scientists have demonstrated the benefits of walking for creative thinking. It can significantly improve certain types of creative cognitive features. Walking can enhance the free flow of ideas. It's not just that we get physical health benefits of exercise but also psychological benefits that can't be overlooked. Walking also encourages the release of the brain chemicals that are responsible for the production of cells in the hippocampus, the part of the brain associated with memory and learning. The hippocampus grows as people get fitter. This, in turn, boosts concentration levels and cognitive ability.

Some studies show that exercise can work quickly to elevate depressed mood in many people. It's so easy to go into a spiral if you are writing about difficult experiences. It's like hoping to heal while picking on scabs, you know? I have a writer friend who once confessed, "Unless my partner and are bouncing off the walls, I can't complete any writing projects." He continued, "Stability is corrosive for my creative process." But then the chosen chaotic dynamics of his relationship quickly increase stress in his life, which hinders his creativity. Exercise may improve mental health by helping the brain cope better with stress.

A 2010 study put participants through eight weeks of daily yoga and meditation practice.[10] The participants reported a reduction in stress. And their brain scans showed) shrinkage in their amygdale. Exercise can have potent effects on our mood. Exercising even moderately boosts endorphin levels, and these feel-good chemicals protect our brains and bodies while reducing the risk of depression. For example, a simple yoga practice can calm your mind. It can help build awareness and open you up to creative inspiration. Yoga can also help reduce stress, improve the quality of your sleep, lower anxiety, and increase the flow of creative juices.

So many writers I have spoken with believe that a good workout is an unnecessary commitment, and it takes time away from their writing. What they don't realize is that staying cooped up inside a room all by themselves can be terrible for their creativity, productivity, and overall well-being.

Working out doesn't have to be overwhelming. Start with an exercise that you're actually excited about. Motivate yourself to get into a regimen of it on a regular basis. Not everyone needs to go for a run at the crack of dawn. You definitely don't need to turn your body upside down to lower stress. Find a time and type of movement that works for you. Once you get those endorphins going and start feeling those creative juices flowing, you will learn to appreciate the benefits of working out on your writing life.

Besides making memories stronger, exercise can help one focus and stay on task. So, get out of that chair! Get yourself moving and you will probably return to your writing with creative juices flowing through every cell.

---

[10] https://pubmed.ncbi.nlm.nih.gov/19776221/

Is Your Perception of Creativity Hurting Your Writing?

> "Through the mere act of creating something—anything—
> you might inadvertently produce work that is magnificent,
> eternal, or important."
>
> —Elizabeth Gilbert, *Big Magic*

I was talking to Day Singh—a friend of mine who is a clinical social worker/therapist, LCSW-R, and has experience working with creative professionals—about creativity. The two of us go for weekly walks amidst nature where we talk about life, challenges, and wins. Both the friendship and our weekly self-care ritual are cathartic.

I confessed to her that on some days, I find the distance between my writing and myself increasing. It's not because of writer's block or some newly developed disinterest in writing. Between managing a job, handling a coaching business, juggling responsibilities at home, and nursing myself back to health, I often don't find myself sitting down with my laptop or scribbling in a journal with a pen.

For most of my adult life, I have woken up at 4:45 am and written for a couple of hours before beginning the workday. Not writing with the same devotion leaves me feeling less than whole on some days.

Day heard me patiently. As we sat down on a bench in the park, she took a deep breath, and said, "Sweta, what's going on?"

"I have contracts for two books, and I haven't been able to work on them," I confessed.

"What do you envision as writing?" she asked pointblank.

"Having written and traditionally published 12 books inside of nine years, I am having trouble grappling with this phase where even putting four sentences together takes so much out of me."

"Have you tried writing for yourself?" she asked.

I looked confused.

She continued, "Writing for the sake of writing, not for someone else."

"What do you mean?"

"Why don't you write about what you are feeling? Like not being able to write?" She spoke affectionately as if I were a five-year-old heartbroken over a broken toy. "Write for yourself. Not to meet a deadline. Not because an editor needs a piece. Not because you need to write 5,000 words a day to finish your book. Write without editing. Write about not being able to make time to write. Write without any premeditated thoughts about what good writing looks like."

A light bulb went on inside my head, and I immediately understood my dilemma. Because of my misplaced understanding of creativity, I had forgotten the joy of writing and as a result started to undermine my own creative abilities. Because I wasn't able to make big, daily chunks of commitment to what I considered creative writing, I was limiting myself and in turn, my creativity.

Ask yourself what writing means to you. Does writing bring you joy? If you are a writer, you will always be one. Merriam Webster defines creativity as *the ability to create*. If you expand your imagination on what qualifies for creative writing, it helps put everything into perspective. A scribble in the journal is creative. A tweet or caption for Instagram or narrative Facebook post that one writes, it's all part of the creative family. As Elizabeth Gilbert wrote in *Big Magic: Creative Living Beyond Fear* "If you're alive, you're a creative person."

Here is what has happened: My life changed drastically in the last year. From suddenly finding myself in the ER, fighting for my life… all of that has had an impact on my body, life, priorities, and creative abilities. From working a day job to rebuilding my body and reestablishing the business, it's been a year of shifting gears, feeling grateful, fighting fears, and rethinking what's most important.

Writing has always found an important place at every stage of my life. Writing feeds my soul. Writing makes me come alive. Writing is how I process ideas and imagination. Writing is how I heal and make sense of the world. But I forgot to extend the compassion I have devoted to my loved ones, colleagues, and clients to myself or my writing. All I saw was a writer not meeting self-imposed deadlines; I failed to see a writer working hard to keep creativity alive and managing to carve out time for her words, sometimes through just 140 characters in a tweet.

Go easy on yourself. Life happens and responsibilities shift. You might not always have the time or energy—despite all the intention—to write a 500-word article or develop your protagonist's personality or dive deep into memory lane to churn out a personal essay or peel scabs off your past to pour out a poem. That shouldn't stop you from calling yourself a writer or from doing any free writing.

I have to say, ever since my friend and I had the conversation about shifting my perspective about creativity, I have been feeling more productive and nourished. The pressure is off, and I get to have fun with words. Gosh, there is something liberating about writing without an agenda or a deadline. The catharsis is real. The creativity is unleashed. And the words all make sense in a much more organic and authentic way.

Let's not pigeonhole creativity, friends. Let no one tell you what makes you a writer, including that inner critic in you.

Why Writing Is a Form of Meditation

I write because writing is how I make sense of my world. When I was eight years old and lived in Libya with my parents, I saw my neighbor and his four wives one evening: the wives sat in the back of his pick-up truck and the sheep sat upfront. When I asked why, I was told that the man believed women, not sheep, were dispensable. I wrote about it. Ever since, good or bad, I haven't known life without writing.

Writing is hard work. There are ideas. Outside influences. Untold stories. Unshared fears. A million thoughts race through the mind. It can be a bloody torture if you don't tame your mind.

But even on days when I question the importance of writing, I write. Those moments when I get frustrated because writing doesn't pay well and I get tired of the hustle, I write. Moments when words betray me or the hurt from sharing stories that open up unhealed wounds gnaw at me, I take to my pen.

Writing is as important to me as breathing. And I wouldn't have understood this connection had it not been for meditation.

Meditation calms the brain. Without a meditation practice, we probably don't tap into the potential of our creative juices. When your nerves are relaxed and your body is happy, you process information the "right" way. Because your brain isn't reacting to outside stimulation, you are more tuned into what YOU want. And the stories you want to share, not what others think you should write about.

Writing is a form of meditation...

Show up

As artists and writers, we know that showing up daily to our work helps. One word. One page. One scene. And you have a book ready eventually. Meditation works the same way. You start with a 5-minute practice. Yes, there is restlessness and fear of failure. Slowly but surely, you develop a daily meditation practice. And the more you meditate, the better you get at it.

Let go off expectations

A few years ago, I wouldn't be kind to myself if I had a bad writing day. I would feel like a failure. That meant I would grab that extra glass of wine or scoop of ice cream and repent it later. Because of a dedicated meditation practice now, every time that I sit on the floor cross-legged, with my eyes closed and focus on the breath, I have no idea what my experience is going to be like.

Some days, I go into such a deep state that I can't hear a word. And then there are other days where the sound of my own breath irks me. Similarly, when I start my laptop to write, I don't sit down to write with any expectations. I am okay with this uncertainty. The minute I take the pressure off myself, my productivity becomes higher.

Maintain devotion

Dr. Vasant Lad, the enlightened Ayurveda teacher who runs The Ayurvedic Institute in New Mexico, taught me the importance of devotion and morning rituals. In case you are wondering, no, you don't have to be religious. But devotion is key to cultivating a solid writing practice. As I burn my incense and bow my head to the "guru," teachers past and present every morning, and start to write after a short meditation, I find faith. In my devotion. In my hard work. In the universe. In my discipline. Also, there is something humbling about bowing my head to no one in particular—just the art of writing. It's such a candid reminder that our words and views are not bigger than the world itself.

Protect your time

I used to be careless with my time. Being helpful is one thing; I was always available, never prioritizing, and showing up to everything. As a result, I never protected my writing time or days. To keep up with my deadlines and my personal life, I would compromise on my sleep. Doing so would negatively impact my health. For almost a year, I would contract a fever every few weeks. Meditation has trained me to find stillness and not engage in the barrenness of a busy life. I don't suffer from fear of missing out any longer. I am present when my friends and family need me. And I am equally present for my needs. I am able to protect my thoughts, my energy, and my writing.

Why Women Writers Need to Empower Each Other

"There is a special place in hell for women who don't help other women."
—Madeleine Albright speaking to the WNBA's All-Decade Team, 2006

Writing is a solitary profession. The stillness and the isolation make for important ingredients in the recipe of writing. That said, no one can survive and thrive in silos forever. Wanting human connection and engagement is part of our nature and need for survival. But it gets tricky because as writers, we are very vulnerable. We have to be doubly careful about the company we keep. We cannot ignore the extreme importance of surrounding ourselves with supportive and compassionate people. For women, building a healthy community of writers, who are compassionate and lift you up, as your support group is even more important.

Research shows us that there is a gender bias when it comes to women writers. Women struggle with their work being taken seriously. The assumption is that for a man, writing is a career. Somehow, the same doesn't apply to women. The common belief is that writing is something women do on the side. Like a hobby. Or pursue something in their free time as rich, bored housewives. Furthermore, Joanne Harris tells us about the difference in perception of female versus male writers. "Women are still viewed as a niche group, dealing solely with women's issues, whereas men (even in the same area) are thought of as dealing with important, universal themes."

The bias permeates through reviews as well. In 2017, *The New York Review of Books*' articles had the greatest gender disparity, with just 23.3% of the magazine's published writers identifying as women.

What can we do to change this in the smallest and biggest of ways?

Build each other up

Encourage other women writers to follow their passions and voice their opinions. Acknowledging the work of a female writer can help shine a light on your colleague's or peer's writing efforts. There's enough to go around—the more of us who are successful, the more we raise the demand for our professions, and we get more book reviews. The more we can demand equal pay within the publishing industry, the more we can dissolve stereotypes engulfing women writers. Stop approaching life with a scarcity mindset. Believe in abundance.

Have each other's backs

Standing up for a woman writer if she is being bullied or trolled online is another way of showing support. If a writer friend or coworker is interrupted during a pitch, you could politely say that she was not done with her story. Buying books written by women writers and sharing their writing/book images on social media is also sisterhood. The concept of women writers helping other female writing colleagues and peers benefits both parties.

Don't compare yourself to others

There is no need for women writers to compare themselves to other women in their field. You are where you need to be. No one can write your story but you. No one can take away what's truly yours. Everyone has a unique voice. Everyone has twenty-four hours in a day. The competition and jealousy are both endless and mindless and can send you into a downward spiral. Instead, use other women writers' success to inspire your writing, promotions, pitching etc.

Don't make assumptions

Everyone has a story and reason for doing whatever they're doing. Don't assume you know someone else's reasons, and don't spread rumors or gossip about as a result. I was at a literary event in NYC a few years ago where a male writer and a woman writer were inebriated during their reading. While I saw a few eyes roll at the male writer for his slurry speech, I heard so many women gossip and talk behind the woman writer's back. So, it seems that unprofessional behavior is pardoned for a man but not for a woman writer. It's common to hear women talk about how poorly they're being treated by men writers, but can we ignore how some women behave with other women? I have read so many Facebook posts by fellow women writers where they talked about how another woman writer was plagiarizing their content. I have been in the exact same place and know first-hand how infuriating and helpless the copycats and plagiarists can make you feel.

We lift ourselves when we lift others. Women are key for empowering and uplifting other women. We can use our strengths to empower ourselves and our communities. If we really want to achieve equal status to our male counterparts as women writers, then it needs to begin with us. Women writers need to support their fellow women writers and empower one another.

Why Winter Is a Great Time to Write

If you look at Mother Nature, autumn is when the leaves start to fall. Letting go is the mantra and underlying message of the season. By the time winter arrives, trees become bare. Winter is a time when nature's energy withdraws back unto herself. We see fewer birds in the sky. Days become shorter. The air becomes crisper and colder. Animals start to hibernate. And the human desire to be outdoors, for the most part, is lowered.

According to Ayurveda, a person is a miniature reflection of nature. Like the plants and animals around us, winter also slows us down. It bares our soul. If you take cues from nature, winter reminds us to take stock of our lives. It represents a time for much-needed restoration. As writers, we all understand the massive importance of pausing, reflecting, and recharging, no?

Winter allows us to find our voice in the stillness. Winter helps us stay in the present moment. Writing requires introspection. Writing urges writers to connect with their inner self. Winter allows us to curl up around books and our own words. All of the above is key to creativity.

Even though winter can be magical for writers and their writing, it's easy to lose sight of this sense of wonder. I know that January-February (Here in the North East) get a bad reputation—the freezing temperatures and multiple layers of clothing are just some of the inconveniences brought about by the cold season. Unless you are into winter sports, these months can feel stifling on some days.

During winter, it seems the world comes to a standstill. But on the bright side: without the distractions of numerous social activities, during winter one can spend time with solitude, which is integral to writing. There are fewer book launches, barbeques, brunches, weddings, literary readings, or other events nudging us to step out, walk away from our writing, and commit to late nights. One can intentionally establish more control over our writing schedule and social commitments. Winter gives the opportunity to discipline our creative habits, so we can meet those deadlines.

Writing demands spending time alone. And doing so becomes so much easier when the world around you is not up in a frenzy. Winter, for a writer, is a time of contemplation and deep thought. It creates opportunities to reflect on the year and experiences. It compels us to sit with discomfort and address those stories that keep us awake at night.

If winter gets you down, you are not alone. But a slight shift in mindset can make the bitter cold months some of your most productive ones. Winter: the season when we can write; we can edit; we can hone our craft. We can learn new techniques to enhance our writing. Winter: when the world around us slows down.

Huddle up. Allow the chai and coffee aroma to permeate the walls of your home. Make room for the words to percolate before the days become warmer and birds return to their homes. And, we humans struggle to carve out writing time amidst the million distractions. Instead of thinking of winter as a cruel cousin, think of it as a silent benefactor who is supporting your creative pursuits.

Does Our Cultural Upbringing Influence What We Write About?

I have always been curious about the world even before I learned to spell the word CURIOUS. Even as a kid, I noticed what most adults missed: be it the nine-year-old in me in India, who witnessed my dark-skinned aunt rub skin-whitening cream on her face daily so someone would ask for her hand in an arranged marriage. Or our neighbor in North Africa, who used homemade wax to strip off any hair on her body to look attractive so her husband wouldn't bring home another wife.

On one of our visits to India, we saw family on my Dad's side. I had recently found out that my *Bua*, Dad's oldest sister, had died in childbirth long before I was born. I felt an innate attachment to this aunt I'd never met; maybe because she was a poet too? My father had shared some of her work with me.

When I visited her husband's/my uncle's house (where the new wife, kids, and others lived), I couldn't find a single picture of my aunt. The family was, and to date is, so welcoming. But it never occurred to anyone how easily they had replaced my aunt's memories behind the cemented walls of their large house with their new family portrait. In the blink of an eye, another woman replaced her, and no one questioned it.

I wasn't even a teenager when I reckoned: women were treated as commodities and a means to a man's needs.

Despite having had the privilege of studying in an international school in North Africa, attending a boarding school in the foothills of the Himalayas, studying in one of the best colleges, and topping the university in my first master's degree program, I wasn't empowered. If anything, I was crippled by my need for outside validation while fighting my frustration on the inside. I wrote poetry to clear the cobwebs growing inside me.

Within a South Asian context, as a girl and a woman, my identity was always tied to a man: someone's daughter, sister, and eventually, wife and daughter-in-law. Despite my progressive and educated family, some archaic beliefs remained. I was expected to pick up "homely" hobbies, so my future in-laws would be happy with my domestic skills. The college degrees and intellectual abilities were fine, but I had to learn the way to a man's heart, which would be through his stomach. Jane Austen and cumin seeds were given equal importance.

Even if those weren't the exact words dictated to me, that was the essence conveyed to most girls from my generation. *An ambitious woman can't keep her man happy.* My aunts, especially on my father's side, were all Ph.D.s and worked as heads of departments at universities. But they won praise not for shattering the glass ceiling at work with their gold medals and by earning a place at the table. What brought them accolades was the fact that they cooked and fed fresh Indian meals to their husbands and children on a daily basis.

A woman was just a tool to help others exist.

How I was viewed by others wasn't my choice. By Indian standards, I was considered light-skinned. One of the meanings of my name "Sweta" is "white." It's supposed to mean *pure,* but many took the literal meaning and said that they were jealous I was *white.* The assumption was my light skin would get me a good groom. And those who believed (inserting sarcasm and calling them *Good Samaritans*) that my light skin shouldn't go to my head, reiterated that I shouldn't take myself for someone beautiful.

I have always prided myself on my brains and ability to feel other people's pain, not my appearance. But it hurt to be reminded that the color of my skin became an open invitation for comments from anybody and nobody. Questioning the status quo earned me the moniker "badmaash" aka BAD. Because of my curiosity and questions, I made people feel uncomfortable. A good Indian girl was expected to accept what she was told and then manipulate the situation to her advantage. I saw friends and cousins do that as a survival mechanism. As for me, I am direct with my communication. Saying one thing and meaning another isn't where I shine.

I always felt like a misfit in India and North Africa, but I couldn't understand why until I moved to New York City and found the space to breathe. It was a place where I was valued, encouraged, and supported for my opinions.

I became an individual with my own thoughts and opinions, for which I wasn't constantly criticized. It was in NYC that I started to meet like-minded people who cared beyond labels, brands, caste, religion, social popularity, and skin color. I had the opportunity to acknowledge and hold a space for my reality: like so many other South Asian women, I too had been a victim of a plaguing patriarchy.

So, that's what I wanted to write about. I wanted to give a voice to those women who didn't have one or couldn't afford to speak up. I started to address equal rights, domestic violence, gender inequality, sexual assault, archaic traditions, and similar issues through my works.

For over a decade, I have written stories, taught workshops, and shared yoga practice to empower women. I have participated in #MeToo marches and been part of progressive, uplifting conversations to support and promote women. Most of my work revolves around women's empowerment and growth and helping people thrive using holistic wellness. But I have rarely written about race and religion unless it enmeshed and fell under the umbrella of feminism and patriarchy. It wasn't because I have been insensitive to color.

When my first book was published, one of my mom's friends looked at the author headshot and said, *"Kitni gori. Sundar."* Meaning "How fair and beautiful." My hard work, childhood dream, and accomplishments were all tarnished with her three insensitive words. To be fair (no pun intended), this lady probably thought she was paying me a compliment: *gori* is a better compliment than bright/smart/driven for a lot of women even today in South Asia.

In India, numerous matrimonial ads carry this message, "Want fair-complexioned, convent-educated, Hindu girl for my son." We have Bollywood celebrities endorsing skin-whitening creams and reiterating white skin as the key to a happy life. People hire servants and make marriage decisions based on a woman's skin color. Racism in India is as pervasive and more nuanced than in the United States.

I have never been blind to skin color. But I didn't feel the urgency to write about race all these years because, in my head, I wanted women to discover their voice and identity before anything else. I wanted them to find equality in their homes, offices, and communities and be treated as human beings. The color of the skin was part of the battle.

But when George Floyd was murdered in broad daylight, something inside of me felt jolted, again. Anyone with any iota of empathy and humanity felt devastated. Four people made a judgment about Mr. Floyd because of the color of his skin. His murder made me realize that racism and casteism are interlinked with feminism.

A woman of lower caste in India often has darker skin. As a result, she has fewer options available—either professionally or romantically. A person of color in America faces similar challenges. What happened with George Floyd triggered those memories from my past that so clearly drew the line between color and hate, between skin tone and injustice. And I knew I had to write again.

Why We Need to Tell More Than One Story About Any Culture

I remember the first time I watched Chimamanda Ngozi Adichie's TED Talk, *The Danger of a Single Story*, it moved me and stayed with me for a long time. I had talked about this very issue to some of my friends but had never heard this point of view with such eloquence.

When a big-name New York City-based agent expressed interest in my work, I saw Adichie's words come to life. He loved my writing but informed me that America wasn't ready for a happy immigrant novel. His requirement: if I wanted him to pursue the project, I would need the female protagonist to be a bit mellow, depressed, and not empowered.

One of the reasons I wrote *Louisiana Catch* is because I couldn't find myself in any of the books that I read. I was frustrated with not being able to locate South Asian novels in bookstores about female protagonists who thought and lived like me and my friends. Either South Asian female characters were all clubbed under the umbrella of women who wore saris, missed eating fish curry, looked up to their husband for confidence, and never embraced America. Or they didn't exist.

It's important to tell the stories that only we can tell. I wanted to tell the story about modern, educated, empowered, flawed Indian women working hard to break the shackles of patriarchy, defining their identity, and sipping wine along the way. I wanted to write a story about good Indian men who show up as equals in their partnerships despite not having been brought up with those values.

I wanted to highlight life beyond arranged marriages and tyrannical parenting. I desired to showcase how so many women emerge stronger than they could ever imagine. I wanted to emphasize the power of friendship across generations. I read somewhere that stories about our experiences, hopes, and fears help break down the power of clichés and stereotypes.

Indra Nooyi, former CEO of PepsiCo and constantly ranked amongst the world's 100 most powerful women, is an Indian immigrant. During her tenure, the company's sales grew 80%. Why wouldn't people want to read stories about her?

Priyanka Chopra Jonas became a common name in America after the show *Quantico*, the ABC-TV thriller series, became a hit. She is an Indian immigrant who moved to a new country and made a name for herself. Maybe the Nooyis and Chopras of the world represent a small percentage of Indian women. But they do hold space and have helped changed the narrative. I know they have given women like me, my friends, and my cousins a lot of confidence to pursue our dreams and be unapologetic about them. Similarly, over the years, Michelle Obama in the White House as First Lady and American television personality Oprah ruling the syndicated daily talk have probably given African American women a deeper boost of confidence and belonging about what they can reach and achieve.

I tried to convince the agent. If we only hear about people, places or situations from one point of view, we risk accepting one experience as the whole truth. But he refused to change his mind. It was one of the hardest decisions to make, but I walked away and chose not to work with him.

"The single story creates stereotypes, and the problem with stereotypes is not that they are untrue, but that they are incomplete," Adichie says in her talk. "They make one story become the only story."

When *Louisiana Catch* was published by Modern History Press and ended up doing really well (I won the prestigious Voices of the Year Award for it), an older PR personality expressed interest and explained her surprise about the strata of Indians I write about in this book. "Your book is beautiful. But the Indians in your book are so affluent," she exclaimed. "Isn't India poor?"

Apparently, this woman had traveled to India when I was a little kid (India and the world have changed so much over the past few decades) to some yoga retreat. The people who live in small-town India and cater to foreign yogis on the banks of River Ganges are diametrically different from those who live in the urban areas of Mumbai, Bangalore, New Delhi, and other metros. They are an equally important part of the stories about India, but they don't represent the country, just as the people who live in skyscrapers in India's metros aren't the face or voice of the entire nation.

In her talk, Adichie reminds us that if we hear only a single story about another person or country, we risk a critical misunderstanding.

It was interesting that the media personality chose to only experience the part of India that catered to her white-savior guilt syndrome. She showed up to a rural area, paid big tips, did headstands, pitied the poverty, and started to believe that she had spiritually evolved by learning to say "namaste." It's similar to a foreigner wondering, "Aren't all Americans gun-loving, racist, obese people who love their happy meals at McDonalds and can't tell Canada from Mexico on the world map?"

My point is, I chose NOT to believe or write one story about the United States or India. It was an intentional effort to educate myself on both the cultures and do the research. As a writer, it's my job to do so. The novel took good 6–7 years to research, write, and publish. In *Louisiana Catch*, the male protagonist and antagonist are both American men. I wrote the characters as if they were human beings in flesh and blood. Their nationality didn't influence how I created them.

Writer friends: it's on us to break stereotypes and share more than one story about a culture, so we can educate the world. While I do write at the intersection of culture, wellness, and women's empowerment, I try to avoid making my writing culturally biased. I will address the hard truths, but I will also show the good. I have Chimamanda Ngozi Adichie to thank for that.

How to Overcome Writer's Block in 5 Simple Steps

If you are a writer, you have most definitely met your worst enemy: writer's block. Aside from the inner critic that wins at ripping apart the writerly confidence, writer's block can be a real catastrophe, too. It can make you question your creative abilities, send you into a downward spiral about your identity, and make you ponder over your future, amongst other things. Writer's block, like the indignant cold & cough, is impartial; it impacts most writers from time to time. Be it because of waning passion or unrealistic expectations or burnout or real-world distractions, most of us get stalled in our creative work.

Getting out of this sterile, uncreative funk is in the writer's hands. While some might think that procrastinating or waiting for the muse to show up or writing only when you feel inspired or wallowing in self-pity or watching nonstop television or making excuses for the dry, uncreative spell might help overcome writer's block, that's not the case. Overcoming writer's block takes a sincere effort. To get out of the funk, you have to take active steps and create momentum.

Establish routine

After months of not being able to write because of personal and professional commitments in life, I open my laptop and a journal. Guess what? Nothing happens. Not even a word. For six days in a row, I show up. I swallow my pride (after having written and traditionally published 12 books inside 9 years, battling writer's block isn't easy for me), embrace my frustrations, and deal with another non-creative day before leaving for work. On the 7th day, I show up to my words and this time, my words transform into sentences and inside an hour, I write this essay. I am not trying to tell you that I am a genius. This productivity is attributed to conditioned response, something I learned from studying Russian physiologist Ivan Pavlov's experiment with his dogs. In a nutshell, whenever the dog heard the bell, he started to salivate. This was an association that Pavlov cultivated. I don't have the luxury of being a full-time writer, so I have been training my mind to make an association when it sees my laptop and/or journal at the same time every day. This is a simple trick to get words moving on the page using conditioned response. The only guaranteed way of overcoming writer's block is by writing. So, create a routine and follow it diligently. Practice. Practice. Practice.

Free write

Ahhh, the power of writing without an agenda, which is also known as free writing. I have to say, there is something liberating about writing without a deadline or any filters. The catharsis is real. You start to see words pour onto the page and morph into sentences and then paragraphs.

Create bullet points on paper for ideas and brainstorming

I always bring a tiny journal with me wherever I go. Writing by hand connects you with the words and allows your brain to focus on them, understand them, and learn from them. Bullet points help to stay organized and work as sunken treasures you can dip into when looking for ideas on a barren day. Writing down ideas in an organized way by hand gives your brain the space to think and concentrate on what you are writing about. Handwriting can be particularly useful during goal setting and brainstorming, because it's slower and more deliberate. It also helps improve memory. Writing entails using the hand and fingers to form letters. Research tells us that the sequential finger movements activate multiple regions of the brain associated with processing and remembering information. Writing on paper also allows us to break predefined formats and layouts.

Change your environment

One other thing that helps me get out of the non-writing funk, aka writer's block, is being mindful of my environment. What do I mean by that? Given that I haven't hit the jackpot yet (inserts sarcastic smile), there is only so much space my New York City apartment can offer. I find parks and coffee shops and trains and make them home to my writing. But here is the deal: I keep each environment sacred to a particular genre. For instance, if my favorite coffee shop in the neighborhood is where I write nonfiction, I would never bring my poetry or fictional writing into that space. If poems pour in subways, nonfiction and fiction stay buried during the commute. Changing the environment can help with creativity.

Walk the block away

Walking offers unique advantages to improve health and boost creativity. My therapist friends tell me that when a creative professional doesn't get to express their creativity, they can get into depression. A nice, brisk walk might be just what you need to stimulate your brain's creativity and get you back in writing mode as walking unleashes creativity. Researchers from Stanford University have found that walking boosts creative inspiration.[11] They examined the creativity levels of persons while they were walking and while they were sitting down. On average, the creativity level of the walking people increased by 60 percent. Walking helps release creative juices along with endorphins. It circulates more oxygen and blood to the brain.

In the end, don't wait for the perfect moment, optimum word, or seamless spot to start writing and overcome writer's block. Start somewhere, anywhere. A few words. Sentences. Paragraphs. Write something. Anything. Definitely don't make excuses or justifications for not writing. Don't be bogged down by perfectionism and eloquence. Start today, wherever you are. It's easier to pick up speed when you are in the habit of writing. You'll be writing before you know it—conquering writer's block and returning to creative work in due course. The idea is to get words on the page. Eventually, the writer's block will become a distant memory.

---

[11] https://news.stanford.edu/2014/04/24/walking-vs-sitting-042414/

How To Bypass Burnout As a Writer in The World Of Social Media

> "A moment of self-compassion can change your entire day. A
> string of such moments can change the course of your life."
> ~ Christopher K. Germer,
> *The Mindful Path to Self-Compassion*

Social media is incredible; it introduces us to writing opportunities, communities, retreats, residencies, prizes, scholarships, and so much more. It helps us connect and communicate with people around the world. It orchestrates new friendships. Social media dissipates geographic boundaries and makes the writing life less isolated. But, like most things in life, social media too comes with its complications.

Research tells us that excessive and compulsive social media usage is linked to depression, anxiety, insomnia, and low self-esteem amongst other health issues. If we don't learn to take care of ourselves, pause every now and then, and stop refreshing our feeds constantly, burnout is inevitable.

Disconnect to reconnect

While Facebook live and webinars and Zoom meetings make it easier for us to RSVP and "attend" more events because we aren't limited by geographic location and time zones, they can also take a toll. Sleeping at odd hours, skipping meals, not getting enough movement, and jumping from one event to another because there are no commute constrictions can have their own consequences. Fact: It's important to pause. It's good to take breaks in between. It's imperative to exercise and eat right. And it's perfectly fine to not attend anything once in a while. When you make the time to recharge yourself, you get back to your writing life, writing community, and creativity with vigor and appreciation. You have so much more to give to your tribe.

Implement gentle rules

Social media has made access to information seamless. It makes life more alluring. You see pictures of your friends at book launches, literary gatherings, and book clubs, and if you perceive exclusion, it can have negative impact on your mental health. Then there is the fear of missing out and the tendency of overbooking your calendar to not feeling adept because everyone else around you seems to be doing better—courtesy of social media posts. Develop a healthy relationship with social media. Don't check social media posts at least two hours prior to going to bed. Don't log onto your social networks first thing in the morning. Maybe schedule your social media posts or use an app that compels you to take breaks. Consider having an editorial calendar in place to plan content ahead of time and allot specific time of the day to use social media. Whatever you do, do not forget to add a nourishing distance between yourself and social media. Sometimes, we need to build boundaries to protect us from our own thoughts and actions.

Figure out your *why*

Social media can be addictive, and it can create a want for instant gratification. Figure out *why* you are on social media—what your goals and expectations are from it. You don't have to be on every social networking channel just because others are on there. Figure out which social media network makes the most sense to you and allocate time wisely. The reality is that the more time you spend on social media, the more you start to seek personal validation through your social media engagement. So, if you share an update/post something about your new writing, book, interview, essay, award, struggles, or wins, and don't get "enough" likes or comments or emojis on your post right away, you might find yourself refreshing the feed obsessively. Then the inner voice gets loud and leads you on the path to self-deprecatory reflections: *People don't like my writing. People don't like me anymore. People aren't happy for my success. They don't think I am relatable, witty, or intelligent. I don't matter. My words don't make a difference. No one will read my work. My career is over.* The writer's mind can be filled with insecurities, doubts, and self-loathing, we have been told by Robert De Niro at an award function in 2014. We tend to make up fearful stories in our head.

Find your community

While it's important to feel that you aren't alone, it's equally important to know that there are different kinds of writers and paths available for your writing career. That said, not everyone will be a good match for you even though they might be the best human being to have walked this planet. For example, if you are a writer with a day job who is feeling anxious about their commitment to the craft and publishing, talking to a full-time writer who has much more flexibility in their schedule and can afford to spend hours online to research options and opportunities might put you in a more vulnerable space. Talk to those who can relate to your situation. Find those in the same position as you in life and build a community.

Embrace tech timeouts

Have you noticed, on some days, you sit down to write with full intention, and then you make the mistake of opening Facebook or Twitter or Instagram or Snapchat or Pinterest on your phone? And there starts the world of mindless scrolling and thumb impressions. On a good day, aside from wasting productive hours, you might not be deeply impacted. But we all have bad days where we doubt our writing, our voice, and our capabilities. On a day like that, it's easy to assume that everyone in the world has a better life than you. Because social media constantly exposes us to idealized versions of other people's lives, we assume everyone is more successful than we are. Fact: Everyone is struggling in their own ways. People only show those aspects of their lives they want the world to believe. Intentionally disconnecting from social media can give you an untainted perspective.

Social media is powerful. Try to use it mindfully, not reactively. While it's important to be an active member of the writing community and support your fellow writers, it is equally important to take care of your emotional, physical, and mental health. Information overload can overwhelm us for the wrong reasons. There is a tipping point for each one of us, after which we end up on the road to burnout.

)

How Writers Can Make the Most of a Pandemic Winter

"You don't start out writing good stuff. You start out writing crap and thinking it's good stuff, and then gradually you get better at it. That's why I say one of the most valuable traits is persistence."

~ Octavia E. Butler

It's been raining nonstop in NYC as I write this essay. I am a sunshine-loving woman and the relentless downpour (we have had a wet week) dries up my creative juices. It makes me unnecessarily mellow and puts out my creative fire. I like being able to go for a walk in the woods or stroll in the park close to home to tap into my inner voice and connect with the stories that matter.

Denial

Being homebound these past few days, I said to my husband, "You sure we weren't transported to London one night while we were asleep?" Nothing seems strange or impossible in 2020. After all, I remember autumn as a crisp and bright season in NYC, not gray and wet like the weather across the pond that our London friends and family complain about. Imagine what winter will be like?

Acceptance

Once I let the rant out of my system, I ordered a few brightening and heating lamps for our apartment. Because either you change your situation (which I can't at this time) or your attitude around it. 2020 has taught us all that so much of our survival and sanity is dependent on our mindset. We are stuck in the pandemic for a long haul, sometimes with awful weather. We can either accept it with grace or fight a battle with no outcome in sight.

Innovation

I can't write on the couch. I can't work on the floor. So, I carved out an intimate corner for my creative work, which is well-lit and has a space heater for my feet to stay warm. It also has close access to the kitchen—literally five seconds—for the numerous cups of chai I need. I, for one, have not returned to working from coffee shops or a co-working space. I don't see writing residencies or writing retreats in my near future. I live in a NYC apartment, so the space is not something you will read about in an architectural magazine. But I love that it's all mine for *my writing*. In this nook, I don't work my day job. None of my virtual speaking engagements or client coaching happens in my writing space. No one else is allowed to sit in my writing chair. I show up here every day with gratitude in my heart.

Meaningfulness

I view this pandemic as an opportunity to connect with our individual selves and society-at-large. It's an unintended but profound mindfulness practice. When the days get shorter and colder and our ability to go out and see people (even if from a distance) is reduced, writers can rely on the company of their words. While 2020 has been brutal and unprecedented, it's given us writers a lot of material to work with. If you feel too close to it, the timing seems uncomfortable, and it makes you anxious, don't start to write. The brain is still collecting information. It's percolating, fermenting, and processing. These are all vital limbs of the writing process.

Association

I also remind myself that writing is like yoga asanas and meditation—you show up daily with dedication without any attachment to the outcome. Some days will be prolific; others will be null. But show up, because having a habit and purpose can help us feel connected. Be fine with all days not being the same. Be okay with not hammering yourself to produce a daily quota of words. Befriend writing on a deeper level. Sit with the discomfort but don't pressure yourself to churn out page after page. Being a writer doesn't just mean tapping away at the keyboard or scribbling in your journal all day. All these experiences will stay with you. When the time is right, you will write. This approach ultimately reassures me that I will always be a writer (whether I am writing a book or being creative with a social media post), so it eliminates any fear associated with my identity as a writer and encourages me to show up to writing daily.

International perspectives

I interviewed three women writers who live in different countries—
Canada, United Kingdom, and the United States—to get their input
on how we, the writers, can make the most of a pandemic winter, no
matter which place we call home.

London-based Sejal Sehmi, IT consultant and UK editor of *Brown
Girl Magazine,* said, "Being in the midst of the pandemic especially in
the winter is sure to arouse a lot of anxiety and uncertainty—much as
what I myself have suffered during the peak of the lockdown. But it's
also a time that these fears can give way to suppressed emotions
which sometimes can only be articulated in words. Make it a point,
at some time in the day, to keep a regular routine of writing
something, anything, even if it's just a Dear Diary moment. Early
mornings, whilst I appreciate it is more challenging because of the
shorter days to come, I feel is the best time to jot anything that comes
to mind down on paper/journal. Once this becomes a routine, your
creative juices in their own time will naturally build something you
will enjoy reading."

Sehmi further suggested something I can't live without either:
"Meditation can play an integral part in having a clear, focused head
and be mindful of looking for creativity even within the four walls we
are surrounded by. We often spend so long seeking inspiration from
the outside world and forget how close to home it actually is. This is
the time, more than ever, to use our words to self-heal and self-
comfort."

Another poignant suggestion comes from Seattle-based Joyce
Yarrow, author of *Zahara* and *the Lost Books of Light* (Adelaide
Books, NY/Lisbon). "When I think about being a house-bound writer
during this pandemic, what comes to mind are the many books
written by authors while serving time in prison. Although the
majority of these 'prisoner-authors' have little in common with me—I
am not a convicted thug, thief, kidnapper and rapist like Sir Thomas
Malory, who wrote *Le Morte d'Arthur*—there are some I greatly
admire, such as Nelson Mandela (*Conversations with Myself*) and
Piper Kerman (*Orange is the New Black*). The bottom line is that I've
always admired people who are able to transcend their surroundings
and create a safe place in which to be creative. Whether we confine
ourselves willingly or are sequestered by circumstance, developing the
ability to visualize and create worlds that we literally wish into being

is a gift to be treasured. And by nurturing our gratitude for this gift, we can not only survive—we can thrive."

Anita Kushwaha, author of *Secret Lives of Mothers & Daughters*, said, "When we went into lockdown here in Ottawa back in March, like so many of us, my creativity took a nosedive. I couldn't focus for long enough to write or even read. After a while, though, writing became my haven from the uncertainty of the world. At first, things moved slowly. But in time, the pace picked up and I even managed to complete a new manuscript over the span of the next five months. (Fast for me.) Now that we're in the second wave of the pandemic, writing has once again become a kind of sanctuary for me, a place where I can go and have at least some control over what happens. My one suggestion? Observe and embrace the changes in your creative process, find new ways that work for you, and cut yourself some slack if you aren't meeting your own expectations in terms of output. We're all living through something incredibly challenging at the moment. Good luck and keep going!"

While we are ALL in the pandemic together, we are still individuals with our own strengths and struggles and hesitations. Figure out what works for you and your creative process this winter.

AYURVEDA & MINDFULNESS TIPS

How to Use Ayurveda to Listen to Our Body's Signals

> "Ayurveda is a sister philosophy to yoga. It is the science of life or longevity and it teaches about the power and the cycles of nature, as well as the elements."
>
> —Christy Turlington

Have you been feeling exhausted, nervous, and achy of late? As I write this essay, the pandemic continues to bring with it tons of uncertainties. Do you find yourself struggling with fear, loneliness, or anxiety? Do you notice a change in your sleep schedule, be it waking up around 1:30–2:00 a.m. to experiencing extreme insomnia? What about your appetite? Do you feel hungry at the same time every day? Or are there days where you can eat six meals and days when you can go without food for 24 hours and not realize it? What about your hands and feet? Are they colder than the rest of your body? Let's talk about what makes most adults uncomfortable but Ayurveda pays a lot of attention to—bowel movement. In this past month, have you noticed a change in your digestion? Are you feeling constipated, bloated, or gassy more than usual?

What if I told you Ayurveda has an explanation for these various symptoms? These are all expressions of *Vata* excess, or *Vata*-imbalance. We will get to this in a little bit. Today, November 13th is Ayurveda Day. I am grateful that Ayurveda has been the guiding principle of my life for a while now. In Ayurveda, body, mind, and consciousness work together in maintaining balance. Ayurveda has positively impacted how I eat, digest, sleep, and function. I have learned that not every yoga *asana* or workout or breathing technique is a good fit for everyone. There is a reason I get annoyed after doing a headstand on a hot summer day.

Because Ayurveda focuses on individual health, not group or community, it seeks out the root cause of an illness rather than just treating the symptoms. For instance, a painkiller isn't always the answer to a headache from an Ayurvedic perspective. Coffee might be an irritant to many instead of being the wake-up beverage. The western obsession with turmeric as being the cure-all drug might be slightly misplaced if your *Vata* is high.

On a deeper emotional level, Ayurveda has helped me stay centered through the roughest periods of my life. I have learned to pay attention to how people, places, and foods make me feel. It's impacted the quality of my relationships and taught me a million ways to keep stress at bay. It's helped me develop a stronger voice and speak my truth. Most importantly, Ayurveda has shown me that self-care is radical and revolutionary, not selfish, because no one can serve others from an empty place.

What is Ayurveda and where does it come from?

Ayurveda is the oldest continuously practiced medical system in the world. The term Ayurveda is derived from the Sanskrit words *ayur* (life) and *veda* (science or knowledge). Ayurveda also translates as knowledge of life.

The purpose of Ayurveda 5,000 years ago was, and is today, to protect the health of the healthy and alleviate disorders in the diseased. Based on the idea that disease is due to an imbalance or stress in a person's consciousness, Ayurveda encourages certain lifestyle interventions and natural therapies to regain a balance between the body, mind, spirit, and the environment.

How does it work?

Ayurveda teaches us that we are all made up of five elements: ether, air, fire, water, and earth. These elements combine to form *doshas* (*Vata*, *Pitta*, or *Kapha*) or constitution. Ayurveda's aim is to understand one's own constitution (known as *Prakruti* in Sanskrit), imbalances (*Vikruti*), and their relationship to the laws of nature to reach a perfect and harmonious balance in our body, soul, and mind. Understanding our constitution plays a major role in how we can live healthy and happy lives. Imbalances are created by a person's environment and lifestyle.

Doshas also crest at different times of the day, periods of the lifetime, as well as seasons. We are currently in Vata season, which is also known as autumn or fall. Vata is made up of two elements: ether and air. The qualities of Vata are dry, light, rough, cold, mobile, subtle, and clear. Think of this way: autumn brings with it some good hair days, right? That is because the air is dry. No moisture means no frizz. Making these connections—isn't it fun?

Ayurveda brings to light how seasons impact our mood, health, relationships, and more. It outlines the healing power of spices and herbs—what is best to eat for an individual, including how and when and how much. It even tells us what foods make sense for every season and that like increases like.

Try eating popcorn on an autumn day and notice how that feels. Popcorn is a "Vata-food"—i.e. it's rough, dry, light, and can create gas and bloating. Experience what crackers feel like at this time of the year. These are expressions of excess Vata. Instead, try eating seasonal, warm, and well-cooked foods and notice how that impacts your digestion. During Vata season, Ayurveda suggests eating more root vegetables (look around; mother nature has squashes and root veggies in abundance at this time) to stay grounded. What we eat impacts how we think. Ayurveda has been talking about the gut-brain relationship for thousands of years. I am thrilled to see western medicine also acknowledge it now.

Ayurveda also talks about the power of daily routine, *dinacharya,* and honoring the circadian rhythm. Most plants and animals are deeply influenced by nature and live by it. Humankind has gotten away from this habit as we have started to work erratic hours, eat at odd times, drink too much caffeine, and ignore the power of a good night's sleep. The pandemic has exacerbated the problem of irregularity. Many people who work remotely have embraced pajamas and the couch as a 24/7 lifestyle.

We forget that the daily routine itself has a grounding and stabilizing effect on the system—*Vata* is irregular and regularity helps it. The daily routine also calms our nerves, and it reminds us to prioritize self-care, irrespective of what's going on in the world around us. No matter what happens, I don't skip my *dinacharya*—be it dressing up for work in the morning (despite remote working) or meditation or being in bed by 10:00 pm at the latest. *Dinacharya* has made all the difference to my mental, physical, and emotional health in 2020. It's influenced how I have navigated the pandemic.

According to Ayurveda, the nervous system is governed by the *Vata dosha.* It regulates higher neural functions such as mental health and behavior. Because *Vata* not only regulates the nervous system but also our creativity, a *Vata* imbalance negatively affects our ability to create.

Creative professionals: when you become anxious, do you feel crippled by the emotion and are you unable to move forward into your creativity until the source of your anxiety is resolved? Ayurveda tells us that if it remains unresolved, chronic debilitating stress is the result. We can feel blocked.

Ayurveda revitalizes you.

We can maintain and promote well-being by being mindful of what we eat, the way we live, what we consume, how we are with others, and the way we handle stress. Instead of constantly chasing the next thing on our list and working tirelessly at odd hours, this ancient healing science reminds us to turn inward, pause, rest, replenish, and connect with ourselves. When we do that, our nervous system relaxes.

Five Tips for Prioritizing YOU—Better Boundaries, Better Balance

> "Boundaries are a part of self-care. They are healthy, normal, and necessary."
>
> —Doreen Virtue

Life doesn't feel easy when you are juggling home, work, family, emotions, teenage angst, and a million other commitments. The majority of women I speak with comment that their days seem blurry and feel like they have zero to minimal time to process their 24 hours. And then there is guilt, which is such a pervasive female trait! Between my clients, friends, and cousins, I have heard the word *guilt* creep into conversations rather often. Guilt about being too ambitious or guilt about not being adequately career-oriented. Guilt about not being good enough mothers, partners, spouses, daughters, friends. Guilt for physical appearances and guilt for relationships that didn't work. The list is endless. Always on-the-go, taking care of other people, many women tend to overlook what they need. Eventually, the stress and exhaustion catch up, because no one can serve from an empty space.

This is why I'd like to remind women that setting boundaries is imperative. For many of us, asserting your boundaries feels uncomfortable. There is a sense of guilt and fear attached to communicating our needs. Setting healthy boundaries in your personal life can eventually do you, your family, and your career good. It won't happen overnight. And it definitely won't be easy. But with practice, you can do it.

Make me-time sacred

Figure out the time of the day that works best for you and carve out 30 minutes on a daily basis for yourself. Be inflexible about compromising on this time unless there is an emergency. You could use it to meditate or nap or read a book or drink a glass of wine or chai or watch Netflix. But it's your time where you don't actively engage with anyone but yourself. Have a conversation with your family about why you need this "alone-time."

Abandon perfectionism.

When NBC-TV Palm Springs interviewed me, I went on air and confessed that I forgot to bring pants with me from NYC. The interviewer laughed. But I laughed harder because being imperfect in that moment felt so freeing. The day before I caught my flight, I was in upstate New York for work during the day and there was a party in NYC later that evening. By the time I got home and finished packing (I am not very good with last-minute anything), the pants got left behind on the chair. Most of us women want to do it all. So many women struggle with this idea of perfectionism. No one can cook three fresh meals a day, show up to a full-time job, attend all extracurricular activities at their kids' school, throw fancy dinner parties, and look like a TV model 24/7 etc. etc. You get my point. Figure out what's most important to you and what can you let go. I listened to a podcast by Dr. Wayne Dyer where he says that perfectionism is also a sign of our fears and insecurities. Dig deeper and ask yourself what the underlying cause of your perfectionism is.

Learn to say NO

We live in a world where everyone wants a slice of your time. Sometimes, it is OK to say NO and prioritize yourself. Learn to say NO to a toxic phone call. Learn to say NO to a chai or coffee commitment. Learn to say NO to a dinner invite. Learn to say NO to what doesn't nourish your soul. Sure, there might be FOMO in the beginning, but you soon realize that being discerning about your time is an act of freedom.

Surround yourself with solid relationships

Find your tribe and love them hard. They are those who lift you higher and support your dreams. Pay attention to the ones who sustain you, the ones who are apathetic, and the ones who bring you down. You deserve better! Why not surround yourself with people who help you become a better version of yourself?

Stop feeling guilty about endings

Sometimes, friendships and relationships end. I don't mean that in a dramatic, confrontational, or aggressive way. Not every ending has to be bitter or emotionally explosive. Sometimes, people, who have known each other for decades, change. Change isn't bad. But pretending that you don't see the change or the fact that you can no longer identify with a person you have known for years is unhealthy for both parties. Every relationship in our lives either teaches us a lesson or becomes a blessing. Learn from them and move on with grace.

Five Simple Tips to Conserve Your Energy and Keep Your Sanity Intact

We have all been in a room where a friend, family member, colleague, or acquaintance has said something mean or inconsiderate, and as a result, they hurt our feelings or irk or depress us. You ruminate over the happenings and that adds fuel to the fire in your brain. Notice if the pattern of your breathing changes when you become tense. Observe if the pitfall begins where you create stories inside your head and get angrier. You probably feel exhausted from the over-thinking.

Here are 5 tricks and tips to help you manage your annoyance, and in turn conserve your energy, no matter the company.

1. Rely on deep breathing

Close your eyes and breathe deeply. Doing so can release both tension and uneasy feelings from your body. Oxygenation of the brain reduces stress. Breathing correctly can release pleasure-inducing neurochemicals in the brain to elevate moods.

2. Focus on the important

It's easy to get caught up in the "How the heck am I going to deal with XYZ at work or the next work event or dinner party?" Tell yourself that nothing is permanent. You have to handle them for a little bit and then it's done. They have no control over you or your life. You are who you are, and their words hold no power over you.

3. Don't attach intention to people's actions

I am not going to give you a morality speech on how most people are nice, and that you should learn to forgive and move on. No. Sometimes it's hard being the bigger person. But I will say that people come from different emotional spaces. Their behavior isn't always a reflection on you. They might be carrying their own baggage that has nothing to do with you.

4. Become mindful of whom you allow into your life

According to Jim Rohn, "You are the average of the five people you spend the most time with." The people we spend time with the most influence the person we become. It's because of the collective sum of the consciousness combined with your personality and individual consciousness. If you hang out with a bunch of pessimists, who believe the world is out to get them and there is nothing meaningful, you will start descending into the tunnel of pessimism at some point. Even if you are initially a positive individual, you will become negative and angry.

5. Protect your energy

Oftentimes, with family and coworkers, you don't get to pick who you spend time with. You can't tell your boss or aunt or a colleague: "You deplete me. Not hanging out with ya." There are certain social expectations you might feel pressured to meet. That said, you can still protect your energy. Don't engage with someone who provokes you. Remind yourself that their misplaced emotions are about them, not you. You always have the option to avoid intimacy with someone who ruins your mental peace. You always have the option to respond, not react.

Truth: you are the only one losing out if you react to every person and in each situation. The person who has something terrible to say moves on to their next "victim" sooner rather than later. So, why should you be paying for another person's immaturity and giving them the importance, they don't deserve?

Five Ayurvedic Tips to Stay Healthy When Traveling

> "Caring for myself is not self-indulgence, it is self-preservation, and that is an act of political warfare."
> — Audre Lorde, *A Burst of Light*

In the world we live in, people are always on the go. As a creative type, your book/art/music can take you to different parts of the world for extended periods of time. As an entrepreneur, the need for learning, meetings, networking, and lead following can surface at unexpected moments. And you have to grab it in all earnestness.

A few years ago, I started to recognize that I don't sleep well in new spaces and places. Travel stimulates me, and my brain doesn't know how to shut down. If I eat the wrong foods or drink an extra glass of wine, it makes me annoyingly alert. My internal circadian rhythm goes for a toss.

As a result of all of the above, I become emotional, hypersensitive to sound, and sleep-deprived.

Why Does This Happen?

Ayurveda says that our *Vata dosha* can go into imbalance when we travel. According to Maharishi Ayurveda and Kellen Brugman,

> "Made up of the air and space elements, *Vata* governs all movement in the body. It's responsible for movement of the muscles, respiration, heart rate, and the flow of thoughts and emotions. These functions have a natural, regular cycle. So, excess movement such as long car rides and airplane travel can upset these functions, causing stress."

However, life goes on and plans emerge, so we need to find ways to cope. Ayurveda has taught both the creative type and entrepreneur in me how to honor my dreams without compromising on my wellness. Here are a few Ayurvedic tips to stay healthy that have helped me with my travels, and hopefully they can help you as well.

1. Sip warm water throughout the day.

It's readily available everywhere and helps maintain the health of the digestive system. *Vata* imbalance can lead to digestive issues like bloating, constipation, and irregular bowel movements. Warm water prevents it. It also releases toxins and helps with blood circulation.

2. Practice mindful eating.

 Despite all the party invites and dinner treats, I always make sure that I have a few simple, warm, and grounding meals in a loving environment. Emotions affect our food intake as well as digestion.

3. Get some alone time

While it's beautiful to be surrounded by loved ones, it's equally important to spend quiet time alone to reflect, introspect, and grow. Even if it's just for 30 minutes a day, I make time for myself—no agenda, commitments, technology, or community. Find quiet moments reading a book or staring into space or strolling through parks or beaches.

4. Celebrate a wellness hour

Love drinking during happy hour? Then you should also have and celebrate a wellness hour. What does that mean? If my travels include spending time with family or friends, I carry my homemade massage oils and herbal cleansers. On some evenings, instead of opening a bottle of wine or going to another restaurant, I give marma massage to loved ones. We still have fun, but people are relaxed, not hyper, at the end of the evening.

5. Practice alternate nostril breathing

Every night, before going to bed, I do a few rounds of this beautiful breathing technique that helps keep the mind calm by balancing the right and left hemispheres. Sit in a comfortable position with your legs crossed. Place your left hand on your left knee. Lift your right hand up toward your nose. Exhale completely and then use your right thumb to close your right nostril. Inhale through your left nostril and then close the left nostril with your right ring and pinky finger. Exhale through your right nostril. Repeat the process for 7–10 minutes.

Thanks to Ayurveda, I now have a mindful living practice that allows me to nurture myself better whether I am in trains, planes, or automobiles. When my health is okay, my productivity gets elevated because creativity and wellness belong together.

Five Ayurvedic Tips to Help You Sleep Better

> "Sleep is the golden chain that ties health and our bodies together."
>
> —Thomas Dekker

As an author, coach, and global speaker, I end up traveling for work a lot more than I'd like. But, at heart, I am a creature of habit and a homebody who likes to wear my pajamas and cook a big meal at the end of the day—you know, a well-balanced lifestyle. For the longest time, there was a constant inner conflict between what my mind and body wanted and what I was able to provide them with.

Change of place translated into poor quality of sleep. I'd have trouble falling asleep later and wake up exhausted. Often, my digestion would get messed up. My health started to deteriorate, my energy levels dipped, and I began to feel more emotional than usual. Writing, as it is, makes you emotional. Throw sleep-deprivation into the mix, and it gets ugly. J.D. Salinger once said, "Poets are always taking the weather so personally. They're always sticking their emotions in things that have no emotions." I became *that* person!

When I started to look around for options to rectify the problem, I chanced upon Ayurveda. Let me rephrase that. I grew up around Ayurvedic tips and wisdom, thanks to my mom, but like a typical teenager, I disregarded her knowledge until I became an adult. By being in harmony with nature's rhythms, we make our body happy and healthy.

Ayurveda has taught me that self-care is vital for good health and well-being. These 5 Ayurvedic principles have made me a better sleeper, and in turn a more mindful and compassionate human being. I hope they help you, too.

1. Get your sleep on

My husband and I were in Mexico over the holidays with my college friend and her family. Everyone teased that I couldn't stay up to watch most entertainment shows, because my eyes would close shut by 10 pm, even though most kids in the audience would be running around. That's true, but I woke up bright and early every morning despite all the vacation indulgences. Because the mind is slow, stable, and dull between 6–10 pm, it is the ideal time for falling asleep.

2. Eat with awareness

It's best to eat your dinner by 6:30–7:00 pm at the latest because as the sun begins to set, our digestive fire cools. Eating early, preferably a light meal in the evening, helps with digestion, which impacts the quality of sleep. Also, remember to eat undistracted—warm foods with no TV or books or serious conversations. Enjoy and acknowledge the aromas, flavors, and textures of the food.

3. Do gentle oil massage

I still remember when one of my Ayurveda teachers gave each one of us in class a sample bottle of oil to massage our feet with at night. I was skeptical at first about the efficacy of it, but a few days later, I was hooked. There are several nerve endings in our feet. Massaging relaxes you, improves circulation, combats stress, hydrates the skin, and ultimately leads to better quality of sleep. Therefore, I carry herbal oils with me on my trips.

4. Breathe right

Prana means life force or breath sustaining the body; *Ayama* translates as "to extend or draw out." Together the two mean breath extension or control. If you are a Type A like me, your mind rebels against shutting down. Simply by practicing as few as 10 rounds of alternate nostril breathing (*Nadi Shodhana*) each day, you can help quiet the mind and calm your nervous system, and as a result, improve your sleep.

5. Embrace self-compassion

Notice how some people leave you feeling blissful after an interaction, while a few might leave you emotionally drained and annoyed? In Ayurveda, health and wellness depend on a delicate balance between the mind, body, and spirit. Before it's bedtime, be mindful of who you interact with, both online and offline. Easiest way: turn off your computer, television, emails, and social media at least an hour or two before you go to bed.

How Spices Can Heal Our Gut, Mood & Emotions— According to Ayurveda

"Because we cannot scrub our inner body, we need to learn a few skills to help cleanse our tissues, organs, and mind. This is the art of Ayurveda."
—Sebastian Pole, *Discovering the True You with Ayurveda*

I grew up in an Indian home where my mother was religious and prayed daily. Her prayers included gratitude for the food we ate and offerings to the deities. My dad taught me to practice my faith the way I saw fit and what felt truest to me. He always maintained that humanity was above it all. No religion or God ever wanted us to hurt other people in their name. That sat with me. I liked the idea of bowing my head down to a deity because it felt humbling and grounding.

I also liked showing up for people and their needs. And when the foodie in me discovered that there were Gods associated with food, who both protected and nourished us, my heart lit up.

Both my parents taught us to serve only as much as we could eat and finish comfortably. "Don't waste food; you are disrespecting 'Bhagwaan,'" (Gods in Hindi) was what we were brought up to believe. This wasn't just because millions of people went hungry every day but also because food is considered sacred in the Indian culture. It's medicinal, and it is considered a source of nourishment. Food brings communities together. It can aid in mending broken hearts. Food can heal our bodies and help us tell stories. Foods tantalize your taste buds, but also provide you with nutrition.

Anyway, because of my love for food and Vedic teachings, I started to pray to Lord Ganesha and Goddess Annapurna. Ganesha, the Elephant God who is the remover of obstacles in Hinduism, also loves food. Annapurna is considered the goddess of food and the kitchen. Her name is a combination of two words—"Anna" meaning food and "purna" meaning "filled completely." I have a small statue of hers in our kitchen, blessing us and the food we eat.

My mother would use a variety of spices in her cooking. She also changed what spices she used according to the season. Lots of fennel seeds, cumin seeds, and cilantro over summer, and more mustard seeds in winter. Homemade Ayurvedic remedies were readily available in her kitchen. Anything related to digestion almost always had ginger in it. A sore throat and cough called for black pepper-based concoctions. Gas and bloating called for using heeng and ajwain.

Turmeric won the vote for anti-inflammatory preparations. She would use a pinch of turmeric, but not in every dish. Let me break a myth for you: eating turmeric in excess isn't the wisest choice. Also, choose to cook with spices instead of eating them in tablet form—it helps with better absorption.

When Ayurveda became the guiding principle of my diet and lifestyle, I finally understood how every meal offers an opportunity to build a better relationship with our body and mind.

Spices influence the foods we eat. And food impacts our gut, our mood, our emotions, and our overall well-being. It is also believed that food can be not only medicinal but also preemptive in maintaining the body's immunity to disease... if we eat correctly.

Ayurveda teaches us that the spice cabinet is our first access to the apothecary. It can turn our pantry into a holistic medicine cabinet. Spices make food taste delicious, sure. But did you know that adding the right spices turns food into medicine? Spices are packed with healing power and can be potent in their effects. One of the reasons spices are revered in Ayurveda is because most spices kindle our *agni* (digestive fire), which enhances digestion. Spices also help remove accumulated *ama* (toxins).

Ayurveda reminds us that proper digestion and elimination are critical for optimal health. Everything we eat will either become the tissues of the body or ama, and the determining factor is the strength of our agni.

When we don't digest food well, it creates a kind of slimy sludge in the gut. Some of us will have reactions like gas and bloating (*Vata*). Others will battle heartburn, acid reflux, or diarrhea (*Pitta*). A few might experience sluggish digestion and the feeling of heaviness (*Kapha*). Spices help to regulate agni, and thus help to ensure that we properly digest the foods that we eat. So, use them liberally in your cooking!

Knowing how to use spices to support your digestion and bring balance to a meal will make it easy to feel healthy in your body and mind. Many of the people I have worked with grew up eating bland food. As a result, their digestion became quite messed up. Ayurveda teaches us that bland food, much like raw foods, is hard to digest. Adding spice doesn't translate into eating spicy foods where you burn your gut and tongue. It means enhancing the taste, quality, property, and aroma of the foods by adding optimal spices.

For every dosha and season, Ayurveda recommends different spices. These are colorful and flavorful ingredients designed for healing, building energy, providing immune support, improving gut health, and longevity.

Ayurveda can return us to balance, health, and vital well-being. Are you ready to open a jar of any spice that speaks to you and soak in the aroma? Spices give us the opportunity to engage all of our senses—not just taste. Look at the colors, the vibrancy. Notice how that makes you feel. Observe what it does to all of your senses. Enjoy delicious spices and know that you're giving your digestive fire an important boost!

PANDEMIC SURVIVAL KIT

How Mindfulness and Discipline Can Help During the Times of Coronavirus

As a society, we are collectively facing the outbreak of COVID-19. This experience and the resulting fear are both unprecedented. People are panicking and consuming copious amounts of news and food. It is evident from personal conversations and also media that so many are taking to erratic eating and sleeping patterns.

With social distancing, self-isolation, remote working, and lockdowns becoming our guiding mantras, we are continuing to become best friends with Netflix and YouTube videos. Let's not forget mindless scrolling on our tablets and phones and constant message notifications from WhatsApp, Facebook, texts, and more.

We wake up and tune into the news, and the last thing we feed our souls before turning off the lights is more updates on the coronavirus. Continually listening to the negativity in the news can disrupt our body and drain our energy. We are subconsciously replicating our offline, pre-coronavirus world into our current online life. Too much noise. Too much mindlessness. Too much busyness. Excessive eating and talking. Uncontrolled messaging and phone time. The universe has forced us to reevaluate how the human race exists.

Use this opportunity to get to know the real you. Discover your purpose. This is a great time to go within. If you can learn to be friends with your own company, you will do well under any circumstances.

When I was a kid, there was no internet or social media. There was the television but with minimal channels and limited programs. In the early days, people in the neighborhood got together at the TV-owner's place. Hopping on a plane wasn't always easy. So, many relied on long trains rides to visit their grandparents during summer breaks. The journey was incomplete without several strategically packed home-cooked meals, small budgets, and frighteningly few entertainment options. As a result, we spent more time with the family and didn't indulge in constant instant gratification.

We were a lot less selfish. We got to know our neighbors (sometimes even during long-distance train rides). We learned to bond with people without considering what they could do for us. The connections were deep.

Those were some fundamentals of life. I think we should focus on the present for happiness, centeredness, and peace. It also supports health and well-being.

1. Connect compassionately

Now is the time to connect with family and friends. Because we are all at home and a lot more rested, many more in your business networks might be more unprejudiced and open to connecting. Deepen and strengthen your existing personal and professional relationships. But be mindful of who you connect with.

Yoga reminds us to hold space with benevolence for others. Yoga also reminds us to protect ourselves from negativity and build boundaries to survive the ordeal. Depending on who is processing their anxiety, don't get caught in the crossfire.

Now is the time to intentionally bolster YOU by surrounding yourself with nourishing company. I remember the first week when NYC went on PAUSE, and we were asked to work from home and maintain social distancing, I must have done Zoom video calls with at least 50 people.

This included friends, family, and colleagues. But by the time the weekend turned up, I felt depleted. I am an extrovert, but I also need a lot of quiet in my life and for my creativity. I cannot chat nonstop—be it on the phone or group chats. The mindless discussions impacted my sleep and productivity. I have learned to pace myself now.

2. Eat attentively

As I have said in other contexts, be kind with what you feed your body. There is a school of thought that tells us that the coronavirus doesn't thrive in the heat. It's simple; eat warm, cooked foods at this time. Ayurveda reiterates no cold drinks or refrigerated foods. Drink warm water first thing when you wake up in the morning as it aids in digestion and expels toxins. Notice if certain foods make you feel better or worse.

Sip on herbal teas throughout the day, if you like. Avoid or decrease your consumption of animal protein and eggs as they are acidic in nature. Alkaline foods, like green leafy vegetables and lentils, boost your immunity, so increase their intake. Include ginger, basil, turmeric, and black pepper in your meals.

3. Rise and shine

Whether or not you have a day job or your own business or a kid you need to help with homeschooling at this point, having a routine in place can be great for your mental health. Rolling out of bed in pajamas and logging into work or passing out on the couch while watching television hardly add any value to your mindset or well-being.

If anything, lack of discipline can be a constant reminder of the scary, erratic world. A hot shower can feel relaxing and positively impact our thinking. Dress up in the mornings. Dressing up can give you a sense of purpose and stability in times when everything feels out of control, and it's hard to keep track of days of the week.

4. Uphold positivity

It's heartbreaking to lose your job and/or loved ones to COVID-19. It's not easy to adapt to this new normal overnight. It's difficult not to be impacted if people you care about are in the hospital because of COVID-19, and you can't even visit them. But know that nothing is permanent in this world. If anything, the only constant is change.

A positive mindset can help you handle all the triumphs and stop you from going into a downward spiral. Be resilient. Know that this too shall pass. Also, know that it is okay not to be okay on some days. It's perfectly normal to experience a range of emotions when life feels so fragile. Pay attention to what makes you happy and lifts your mood. Music. Books. Meditation. Focus on what's working for you versus what isn't. Including gratitude in your life can shift gears and show you there is always something to be thankful for. When I was in severe chronic pain, the top item on my gratitude list one night was, "Hey, today the pain never went above 7/10!"

Spend time at home without complaining. There are people who don't have homes or meals or jobs or health insurance or health. If you have the luxury to feel bored, think about them for a moment.

5. Movement is medicine

While it's easy to hide behind a box of cookies and not feel motivated to do any workouts or include any daily movements, you should be doing quite the opposite. Most of us partake in emotional eating when stressed. If you aren't moving, you are probably not mindful of your health.

The last thing you need is lifestyle-induced diseases caused by increased calorie intake (from refined sugar and alcohol) and no exercise. Moving your body is imperative for your mental health too, as exercise releases endorphins, which can help bring about feelings of euphoria and general well-being.

Daily yoga and pranayama practice can lower stress, boost your immune system, and strengthen your respiratory system. Pranayama can keep your nasal passages very clean. Meditation can help you stay focused, centered, and grateful. Pay attention. Cultivate mindfulness. Following your *dinacharya* (daily routine) and aligning yourself with the circadian rhythm of the universe during this mayhem can help you stay healthy physically, emotionally, and spiritually.

How Do You Keep Creative Writing Alive in The Time of Coronavirus?

> "It doesn't have to be amazing; it just has to be authentic."
> — Elizabeth Gilbert

Writing is a solitary profession and writers are labeled as folks who like to live inside their own creative cocoon that they rarely leave. But I'd like to clarify two things.

Not all writers are introverts. And there's nothing wrong with being one. You should value who you are and what works for you. I want to point out that many of us writers thrive on the energy of the people around us. We are conversation starters, people-person, gregarious, friendly, life-of-the-party, and bubbly. Once in a while, we might like our peace and me-time. But, for the most part, we love being amidst people. That's how we feel charged and inspired. Sure, we keep our writing time as solitary because there is no easy way to connect to your inner voice if there is distracting noise outside. But other than that, we like to surround ourselves with invigorating words and company. Making a choice to limit your social interactions, putting yourself under quarantine to finish deadlines, and working from home in your pajamas is one thing; being unable to step out of the house and see people because of a community-wide threat caused by coronavirus is a whole other ball game.

When the first wave of "work-from-home" rumors began and people started to wear masks in the New York subways, I knew it was time to pull out my yoga clothes and pack up dresses because remote working was unavoidable for the foreseen future. I pulled out my Type-A, New Yorker deadline cards for new articles to pitch and write and also came up with a timeline for my new book. I figured that after finishing my day job, I would easily go for a walk or run or practice yoga at home in the evenings, cook a hearty dinner for the family, and then work on my writing projects.

I mean, I typically wake up at the crack of dawn to write before I leave for work. I also write in the subway—on my way to work and on the way back. On some days, I replace writing time with reading. Now with the long commute out of the picture, I figured I had a few extra hours on a daily basis. Time to get those productivity fingers going at full speed!! I could easily finish the book by the end of March. WRONG!

Social distancing is imperative at this point to keep ourselves and the world safe. I like to think of myself as a socially conscious and responsible human being. So, even before the government made it mandatory, I canceled our social plans and the workshops I was scheduled to teach. I didn't want to endanger anyone's safety. That's the only way to flatten the curve and stop the spread of the disease.

But can we pause for a minute and acknowledge the loneliness and overwhelm that self-isolation creates for many of us? I love being able to chat up friends, family, and colleagues on video calls on a daily basis these days, but can we overlook the power of sharing meals, smiles, and ideas in person?

With remote working and families being at home, the list of chores, number of meals, and frequency of grocery shopping as well as cleaning have all gone up. I would like to reiterate that I am not complaining, just acknowledging that our world and life as we knew it have changed overnight. And that might have impacted our creative process.

There is so much uncertainty and anxiousness surrounding us. I have shared before that I wrote an award-winning collection of poems, *Saris and a Single Malt* about my mother inside of a week. But creating from a place of grief and brokenness is very different from writing from a place of fear and anxiety. When the world is worried about toilet paper, groceries, and basic survival, it's hard to dive deep into the crevasses of creativity. How do I create a fictitious world in my novel when the real world around me is falling apart?

Despite my daily yoga and wellness practices, I don't feel as centered. My writing space is the same as the place from where I do my day job or take client video calls. With no separation between my day-to-day and creative life, and no solutions available in the next few weeks (maybe months?) until the pandemic settles down, I decided to reroute my thinking and work from a place of acceptance. Accept that these are unusual times, and I don't want my creativity to feel the pressure of Pavlov's dog experiment—when I show up to the computer, words must pour.

I decided to pause. Take each day as it comes. Observe the words that want to be written but not judge them. Pay attention to the stories I want to tell versus the ones I think should be told. On my solitary long walks, I started to tune into what my heart and gut were indicating. The minute I took off the self-imposed pressure, I realized that I wanted to write essays on wellness, because what the world needs right now is a lot of compassion, accurate information, and tips on how to take better care of us—be it physically, emotionally, or mentally. I have had people ask me about Ayurvedic lifestyle and cooking tips to help boost their immunity and keep their mental health nourished.

The more essays and articles I am called to write on the role of wellness, productivity, and creativity—specifically in the time of coronavirus—the more my creative juices flow with ease. It's as if they know this is what they need to create at this point. Little did I realize that I had started off with a rigid deadline for a novel but ended up with opening up an old project only because I decided to let go and stopped to manipulate the direction of my creativity.

Writing life in the time of self-quarantine and social distancing can feel unexpectedly dry, different, and disappointing at times. If I may suggest, use this time to pause, ponder, and find your purpose as a creative professional instead of pressuring yourself to be a productivity machine churning out pages. The new book won't go anywhere. This might be the time to figure out your authentic voice and consider if it's time to innovate or branch out as a writer.

What Self-Isolation During COVID Has Taught Me About Creativity

The first week of NYC going on PAUSE, I felt something inside of me die. Don't get me wrong; I was and continue to support remote working and social distancing to stop the spread of the virus, even on days when self-isolation makes me feel desolate. My mind has been in agreement with Governor Cuomo's stance for the state of New York. But my heart has continued to feel heavy.

Initially, knowing that we wouldn't be able to see anyone for an unknown period made me anxious. Conversations, engagements, discussions, chai-time, happy hour, book launches, literary events—don't they all impact our writing? No subway rides or any form of travel—home to several of my stories and inspiration—sounded scary. I get my writing done during my commute to work. But when your commute involves walking from your bedroom to your living room in a New York City apartment—your tiny, temporary, makeshift office until such time you can return to our original, physical spaces—it's hard to feel jazzed up about storytelling.

I told myself I couldn't conjure up creative ideas and build a fictional world for my new novel when the real world around me was crumbling. Everywhere I turned, someone was sick, dying, losing their job and home. Was my family, which is spread across three countries, safe? What could I do to ensure my friends, family, colleagues, and I stayed healthy without jeopardizing anyone's safety or undermining anyone's beliefs? Not having answers or having any control can be incapacitating.

There have been nonstop rumors and misinformation about the virus, which has left most of us feeling overwhelmed. For instance, walking is integral to my creative process. Some advised, get in that movement every day while others recommended not stepping out of the house. One day we were told to not wear a mask; next thing you hear was that masks are the best thing since sliced bread. You can't help but wonder, *Crap, did I catch the virus because some fools couldn't make up their minds?*

The need for food has been tied into our survival instincts. Working from home and not being able to dine out means being creative in the kitchen at least twice a day, so boredom doesn't set in. Then there was creativity involved in food shopping. Would Instacart deliver groceries? Back up; would I even find a slot to get stuff delivered at home? Will all the items we ordered be available? How would I creatively use two pounds of jalapenos the store delivered as a replacement for the green peppers? Were we being doubly conscious not to over-order so there was enough available for others doing their food shopping?

The brain has been working overtime: learning to survive, separating good information from bad information, and processing one day at a time. The array of human emotions can be exhausting. Writing requires centeredness. But COVID-19 has washed away every iota of calm. There is the uncertainty of not knowing whether your job exists; the guilt of surviving and having a job; the fear of closing down your business or the guilt of receiving funding for your company when those around you didn't. It is stressful not knowing whether your family and friends working on the frontlines of the healthcare system are safe or not. I have the privilege of being able to work from home when so many essential workers don't have the option and risk their lives daily to keep us safe. The annoyance you feel when people don't wear masks and hang out in big groups in public spaces. Switching between gratitude and trepidation on a daily basis can dry up your creative juices.

While you might not have the energy to pen down your thoughts or complete that next project, it doesn't make you any less of a writer. The experiences are sinking in, deep into your core. They are marinating and ruminating and blending and fermenting. When you are ready, these ideas and thoughts will take the form of words. They will pick the genre they want to be written in. I would like to remind us writers that we have been continuing to stay creative; just not in the way we traditionally perceive creativity. We forget that words are secure; they know how to carve room for themselves in our lives. We, as writers, need to have a little more faith in our relationship with writing.

How can I be so confident? Remember when I fell ill in 2018? Writing is how I have always made sense of the world. But my world turned upside down, and I barely managed to stay alive. Being homebound for six months made me vulnerable and forced me to ask difficult questions: were writing and I over because I was physically unable to write? Would it become an unrequited relationship where words wouldn't want to see me? But here I am today, sharing this essay with all of you.

My health scare in 2018 taught me several lessons. One of the biggest was in patience and faith:

Writing, much like biking and yoga, is something you don't forget. This doesn't have to be the time to catch up on your writing. It might take some time to reconnect, but once a writer, always a writer. Wait. Breathe. Pause. Reflect. Breathe. Writing is about showing up daily with dedication to your words. Yes, we want the muse to inspire us. But if she declines to join, you'll still be fine. Because perseverance, discipline, and dedication beat a moody muse any day.

We will be okay. Words. Us. Writers. Writing. So many writers are putting an insane amount of productivity pressure on themselves. This time of PAUSE/ lockdown/ shelter-in-place has given us the opportunity to sit with ourselves. It has taught us to never take anything, including the mental space for creativity, for granted. Most importantly, it has offered us the opportunity to explore what we write and what we really want to write about. Reacquaint yourself with writing. That's huge!

You can't rush healing or creativity. They happen in their own time. Over the last few weeks, I have heard my friends, who have never written before, say that they feel they have a book in them. My fiction writing colleagues have admitted to dipping their toes in the pool of the nonfiction world. Reality is that the coronavirus, much like any untoward experience, has left us all with stories to tell. Just because you didn't finish writing those stories yesterday doesn't make you any less of a writer. Use this time to process your feelings, sit with your experiences, and connect with your inner voice. Move forward in a manner that is consistent with your life goals and enables your mental health and overall wellness.

Finding My Calm, in The Storm Of Coronavirus, As a Chronic Illness Survivor

I am writing this essay in spring of 2020—in the early days of New York's first wave. These are difficult and confusing times. I don't have to tell you that. Everywhere you turn, there is an update on coronavirus. We wake up every morning to the news of the COVID-19 negatively impacting our lives and well-being. Deaths. Higher incidence in certain geographic areas. Increase in numbers of those affected.

What doesn't help is the plethora of information out there. Not all of it is sensible or reliable. Anxiety has found a home in all of our minds. Social media makes it easy for people to share information but how many of them are truly mindful or knowledgeable about what they post online about a pandemic like coronavirus? Do they check themselves to make sure that they are not contributing to the mass hysteria?

I am bombarded with "How to take care" of myself information in times of coronavirus because I am a chronic illness survivor. I'd like to believe most people mean well, but I also firmly believe that a larger majority don't process every thought that leaves their brain and enters their mouth. In times of instant gratification, impulse often drives what people post on social media or how they craft their messages.

I know first-hand what containment and social distancing mean—my illness rendered me immobile for months. Last year this time, my body was still healing from surgery and months of being homebound. My mind had fought equally hard to avoid depression. My doctor and surgeon were amazed at the quality of my mental health. I had lost my ability to eat, sleep, and walk. I saw seasons change through our living room windows. I missed every family function, holidays, celebrations, friends' successes, my own literary events, book readings, and workshops I offer my clients. I lost clients and my career. Once again, containment and social distancing weren't my choices or doctor's orders, but my body failed to function, so the choice was made for me.

Trust me, many of us chronic illness survivors know what illness can do to your mindset. It's a lot of hard work to find and focus on one ray of sunshine when everything around you seems dark and bleak. It's not easy to go from living a regular life (in my case, winning one of the most prestigious awards for my novel *Louisiana Catch*) to finding yourself in the ER, and suddenly fighting for your life. No signs. No symptoms. And you find yourself in the most horrific situation.

I have made self-care a priority in these times. I have been trusting Ayurveda to help me stay grounded and boost my immunity. I have been relying on the ancient healing science of life to navigate these bizarre times.

Make yourself a priority

Ayurveda teaches us that compassion that doesn't include you isn't true compassion. I have chosen to not read or respond to messages where people share unsolicited advice about surviving coronavirus as a chronic illness survivor. They read something online, start to panic, and pass it down to me. I am sure there is warmth and love behind their action, but I don't need to be reminded that my body is susceptible to falling sick again. As a chronic illness survivor, like many others, I know what frailty of life means. I don't need to be retold that chronic illness survivors are more vulnerable to coronavirus as I watch and read the news too. I don't need to be reminded that my body is weaker than other people's. I work hard to keep it strong and going.

Don't forget to sip on warm water

When I wake up in the morning, one of the first things I do is to drink warm water. I continue to do so throughout the day, because warm water detoxifies the body and lessens any congestion in the chest. It's also known to aid digestion and decrease stress levels. I can't emphasize enough why warm water is medicine for the body.

Get playful with spices and herbs

Ayurveda addresses the importance of spices and herbs in the stages of prevention, maintenance, and healing. I have been cooking most of our meals at home with organic ingredients (whenever possible) and using turmeric (anti-inflammatory and antioxidant), cumin (reduces toxins and helps with indigestion), ginger (eases cold and reduces inflammation), and ghee (anti-inflammatory properties). Our kitchen cabinets can be powerful adversary to all kinds of ailments.

Bend so you don't break

Yoga is my anchor. If I don't have the time for a 60-minute class, I will at least practice it at home for twenty minutes. But my daily practice is important to me. *Surya Namaskar,* or sun salutations, build up heat and boost immunity. According to Ayurveda, sun salutations can also aid in digestion, improve heart health, and unwind the mind and body. It can calm the nervous system.

Connect with your breath via *Bhastrika Pranayama*

(Bellow's breath) is the process of rapid inhalation and exhalation, which gives a boost to the body. Sit in a steady, comfortable posture with the spine straight. Take a few deep, even breaths, letting the abdomen expand as you inhale. When you're ready to begin, exhale by contracting the abdominal muscles quickly and forcefully and follow it with a quick diaphragmatic inhalation, letting the abdominal muscles relax completely. It has beneficial effects on the digestive and respiratory systems and is called the yogic breath of fire. It can help drain out excess phlegm from the lungs and mucus from our respiratory system. It's known to purify the blood and relieve inflammation in the throat. *Bhastrika* also calms the mind. *Bhastrika* increases intra-abdominal pressure and may not be appropriate for women during menstruation or pregnancy or for anyone with an ulcer, hiatal hernia, chronic constipation, heart disease, or high blood pressure.

Spend time self-reflecting

In all of this mayhem, we have control only over our thoughts. We have a choice to fall prey to the plethora of information and hysteria. We have the option to make mindful choices and pay attention to what leading health authorities share but not give into the madness. Meditation can be your best friend in these trying times of uncertainties. It lowers anxiety, enhances focus, reduces stress, increases self-awareness, and calms the mind.

Learn about the healing powers of essential oils

I burn *dosha*-specific (Ayurveda speak) essential oils in diffusers in our living spaces— mostly lavender, geranium, lemongrass, and frankincense. They help relax and soothe the mind. Some oils lower anxiety and aid in digestion. I also blend body massage oils with high-grade essential oils.

My point: While it's important to take care of our physical health in these times (practice good hygiene and be pragmatic about what you feed your body), it's equally important to nurture your mental and emotional health without giving into the frenzy. Trust your instincts, use your common sense, and make informed decisions.

Mental Health & Creativity: How Yoga can Transform your Life & Writing

> "Yoga does not just change the way we see things, it transforms the person who sees."
>
> — B.K.S. Iyengar, *Light on Life*

I have always liked movement and speed. Like a true New Yorker and high *Pitta* individual (Ayurveda would describe as a motivated and driven woman), I am a doer who is hungry for more and onto the next thing by the time I meet one deadline. *Rest is for the weary* used to be my philosophy for many years.

The first time my father suggested that I learn yoga, I said to him, "But isn't that something old people do? Twist their bodies into weird shapes?" Granted I was young, naïve, and ignorant. But the truth is, when I was a little kid, not many youngsters practiced yoga. My *nana*, Mom's father, was the one person I knew who had a diligent daily yoga practice. But *Nana* was old, so I assumed I would learn to contort my body when I aged. Also, when you are younger, you are far more impressionable. Unlike Bollywood celebrities and sportspeople spreading the wisdom about yoga these days or a gazillion wisdom pieces on the power of yoga for creativity, we didn't have that growing up. There were no yoga studios or athletic brands reminding us to be bendy and breathy.

In 2006, I was attending graduate school at Columbia University, running the marketing department of a large accounting firm, managing home, and simultaneously making time for writing and life. I was way over my head. I noticed that my dancing, swimming, cardio, and strength training kept me fit and agile, but my mind felt like a nomad in search of unknown territory. Constantly wired and mentally tired, my sleep started to get impacted. Increasing my daily *chai* intake didn't help either. My writing started to feel less fluid.

I panicked. What would I do if I couldn't write? I see the world through the lens of writing. Eventually I pulled a nerve in my neck due to stress, and it left me bedridden for extended periods of time. At one point, my doctor suggested that I would need to undergo spinal surgery.

Both my father and husband suggested I give yoga a try. I was reluctant at first because I believed yoga was too slow for the Type A New Yorker in me. Pausing, slowing down, and reflecting are what I needed but didn't know at the time. I had no idea that mindfulness and intentional breathing would light up my creativity. Connecting the mind, body, and breath helps us to direct our attention inward, and that is a boon to the creative juices. I wish I had known about this secret sooner.

Yoga combines postures, breathing, and meditation. By the end of my first yoga class, I found a bit of stillness. I didn't quite know how to describe the feeling, but it was like nothing I had experienced before. I didn't know that when I finished practice, I was on a "yoga high." I raised our levels of endorphins and reduced the amount of cortisol, the stress hormone, in our bodies.

Studies have shown that practicing yoga is an extremely effective way of raising endorphin levels. Endorphins create a sense of bliss. In those sixty minutes, my mind had stopped multi-tasking, planning for the upcoming week, or generating a grocery list. It stayed in the present moment. Deep breathing felt rejuvenating. I had felt stuck in my writing—both my thesis and creative writing—but this yoga class led to a humongous release.

Yoga really does have the power to transform your writing

Ideas started flowing freely almost from the moment I started my practice. Over a period of time, with a consistent yoga practice, I felt a shift in my attitude toward creativity. I noticed that the ups and the downs of the writing process didn't plague me. In the way, I started to accept that my body would feel different on any given day. I started to accept rejections and selections as a real part of writing life, not a mourning or celebration of my creative abilities. I started to show up daily to my craft and the yoga mat with no expectations, and 100% dedication. Words started to flow through the creative faucet. On a physical level, I didn't have to undergo surgery; yoga made my neck stronger and released the stress. I can now do push-ups and downward dog with my 50-pound niece sitting on my back.

When I asked Kerry Bajaj, author of *Sleep, Baby, Sleep,* how yoga impacts her creative life, she said, "As a writer, my body can be affected by too much sitting, and posture is affected by hours hunched over at the laptop. Yoga is a lovely counter-balance! During lockdown, I've been doing a lot of restorative yoga and sun salutations. I practice outside, usually in the late afternoon. It's a good way to connect with nature, move my body, release stress, and stay flexible. One of the hardest parts of coping with the 'new normal' is coping with ambiguity. I find that my yoga practice is a helpful reminder to embrace *anitya*, i.e. impermanence. That teaching was always there, and it was always grounding—but never so important as it is now!"

What is the connection between yoga, writers, writing, and mental health?

Creativity and its link with mental health have always been much speculated about. In the largest study on this question, researchers found writers to have more than double the risk of schizophrenia and bipolar disorder compared to a control group of accountants. Writers also faced a greater risk of depression, anxiety disorders, and substance abuse.

Research shows that yoga not only has the power to keep our bodies strong and supple, but also has positive effects on the brain.[12] Yoga can help boost moods even more than walking. Physical balance in asanas follows mental balance and that follows inner calm and resolution, which is again amazing for a writer's mind.

When I asked Jennifer Kleeper, *USA Today* bestselling author of *Unbroken Threads*, about her relationships with yoga, she said, "My mind is in the business of chasing—information, understanding, responsibilities, obligations. This can help my writing, as when bits and ideas I've gathered flutter together in just the right way. But distraction is a *constant*, and sometimes it's hard to reset. I'm fairly new to yoga, but I've found attending the class to be one of the few moments when my mind clears. It's one of the few moments when I'm not pulled to 'look that up,' or 'jot that down.' During our pandemic lockdown, I was fortunate that my favorite yogi led classes live online. Taking her class, hearing her say my name, gave me a sense of normalcy and that opportunity to get my head out of the business of chasing and back into the business of the moment."

Practicing yoga has a powerful effect on our hormones. Yoga can boost dopamine levels, a hormone and neurotransmitter, and as a result, impact our writing.

---

[12] https://www.ncbi.nlm.nih.gov/pmc/articles/PMC4428135/

"Yoga has been my savior for around 15 years. I started practicing it in my mid-twenties. Whereas then, I felt the physical effects, I've really felt the mental benefits during lockdown. My morning routine sets me up for the day with a Zen-like feeling and keeps me sane in a world of chaos. The *Vinyasa* flow I like to practice has helped keep my body from missing the gym too much! I have also been working on the first draft of my novel and have written in that how yoga has helped the character with anxiety, something which I didn't think about before lockdown," says Priya Mulji, Senior Columnist, *Eastern Eye* (Britain's number one newspaper for Asian news).

I have tried to make yoga (asana, pranayama, and meditation) a part of my daily practice for over 15 years. It has changed my life for the best. In nine years, 12 of my books have been published traditionally, and I have won several awards. The reason I say this here is not to brag, but to share with you that I owe a lot of my success and emotional stability to yoga practice, both on and off the mat. Yes, I bend, so I don't break. But yoga also makes me a compassionate and prolific writer.

Gratitude: The Balm We All Need Right Now

During this time of global upheaval and uncertainty, there is much to be gained from the saying by Aesop: "Gratitude turns what we have into enough." We are all grieving at this time in our ways, for our own reasons. Our worlds have turned upside down. We were living our lives and then everything that we knew changed.

According to Elisabeth Kübler Ross & David Kessler, there are five stages of grief: denial, anger, bargaining, depression, and acceptance. When my mother died, I found myself in the anger phase of grieving for an extended period of time. Because she died suddenly, I didn't get to say a goodbye and was left with the burden and pain of unsaid words. Struck by an insurmountable amount of grief, I felt angry. Other members of my family were heartbroken, too, but they expressed their pain differently, and perhaps, because of this, they reached the stage of acceptance a lot sooner than I did.

Over the years, I've realized that we all grieve and heal differently. While my mother's sudden demise left me entrenched in the anger phase of grieving, with the coronavirus pandemic, I reached the acceptance phase inside of two weeks. Why have I been able to evolve through the stages of grief so quickly? Because since the time of my mother's death, I have become best friends with gratitude.

To be clear, using the word "gratitude" and feeling it deeply inside in your core are two separate experiences.

Before my mother passed away, I would express gratitude for measurable moments—be it a two-week vacation or a promotion at work or a table at a restaurant I'd been wanting to try. Thanks to yoga, I now understand and accept that gratitude is what sustains us: The breath that we have, the moments we spend with loved ones, the memories of those deceased, the ability to buy groceries and eat, the capacity to go for a walk, the intention to show up on the yoga mat, and so much more.

As I write, my home city is considered the epicenter of coronavirus in the United States. So many of my close friends are sick with COVID-19. Many of them are on the mend, and I feel grateful for these small mercies. On an average, I receive over a dozen messages from friends and family asking about my family's welfare on a daily basis. So many people urge me to stay within our apartment, not even going for a solitary walk while practicing social distancing, because they are scared of me getting infected. I have gratitude to have people who care about my well-being at a time when everyone is feeling inundated.

Amidst this coronavirus crisis, people are connecting with their families and friends on a deep level. Healthy relationships and meaningful conversations are integral to our survival and mental health. I now do a morning video chat with my dad and check in with my mom-in-law. We have random, hearty conversations that uplift us all. These were the kind of things that were overlooked when we are all running around and living our busy lives.

I have immense gratitude that this pandemic has given us the chance to pause, reflect, and focus on what matters most.

I am a small business owner. My business, like that of majority of other entrepreneurs, has already suffered tremendously. Coronavirus has bludgeoned my livelihood; all of my creativity and wellness workshops and speaking engagements have been postponed until further notice. At this time, the early stages of the pandemic, we are figuring out what virtual teaching/learning would look like. But despite all this upheaval and uncertainty, I am grateful because I believe that if I built my business once, I can build it again.

I know that I am not alone in my suffering; the entire world is a mess. Yet I am grateful that I am surrounded by a community of compassionate colleagues willing to work together to get out of this chaos. I am grateful that we are able to support each other when we hop on Zoom calls to talk about our struggles and our hopes for a brighter tomorrow.

I am not diminishing the challenges anyone is facing during this pandemic. But there is a lot to be grateful for even as we are on lockdown inside our homes. I am *not* suggesting that we should be grateful that the pandemic has consumed our lives, but I am grateful to realize that the only thing that's under my control at this point is my thought process.

One thing that has helped me stay sane these past few weeks is focusing on what I have versus what I have lost.

There are people who don't have jobs, food, healthcare, or access to getting tested for COVID-19. There are people who have lost friends and family to the virus. There are people who are stuck abroad because of travel restrictions brought upon by this virus. I remain grateful because I have a home where I can safely stay with my family. I have access to food to feed myself and my family. I have Internet access to connect with friends and Netflix. If you can work remotely, be in gratitude. If you have a healthy body, be in gratitude. If you have a partner, friend, colleague, family member, or pet who makes sure you are okay, be in gratitude. We will survive... and thrive.

The Key Ingredient for Emotional Healing: Forgiveness

Human beings are complex characters. We have all been hurt, and we have all hurt someone. It might have been unintentional—I'd like to believe that kindness and humanity still exist in the world—but the trauma can't be denied.

We all have wounds. Some of us are aware of their gaping size, while others are in denial about theirs. Such people roam around in the world with their brokenness and pour that into other vulnerable beings. It comes out in the form of physical abuse, emotional abuse, lies, deceit, manipulation, jealousy, anger. Well, you get my point.

December 2020 felt heavy. Not just because the holiday season in the year of the pandemic was different and we were surrounded by suffering instead of loved ones, but also because I uncovered that I hadn't forgiven a few people as they repeated their caustic behavioral patterns during the holiday season. I didn't want to feel so deeply, but I couldn't let my mind disconnect completely. Gosh, I felt like a prisoner of my emotional baggage.

Secondly, in December 2020, I emailed the manuscript for this book, *A Piece of Peace*, to my publisher. The book, as you know, is a collection of essays that acknowledges my illness, the journey to recovery, and the person I have become as a result of it. Writing and revisiting my experiences triggered me on a deeper level.

Two Decembers ago, in 2018, I was in the hospital undergoing a complicated surgery for a chronic illness that showed up suddenly in my life out of nowhere. Several of the doctors I have spoken with and the articles/studies I have read all acknowledge the role of stress and trauma in chronic illness. The timeline: when I fell sick, how it happened, what led to it, who contributed to it all, the manipulations, my struggle with life and death... the whole nine yards came flashing in front of my eyes.

Marc David in his book, *The Slow Down Diet*, talks about the power of forgiveness. He writes, "I'm still amazed at how they who've had long-term eating disorders, chronic fatigue, digestive complaints, and a host of debilitating symptoms see miraculous relief when forgiving people from their past and present."

When I fell sick, I was seething and wanted "justice" from the universe. When people hurt us grievously, we feel the urge to get even—emotionally, mentally, or physically. We might even declare that we have the right to do so. How could I be sick when I tried to be a good person and led a mindful life? How could those who hurt me be healthy and happy when they were a big reason I found myself in the ER, fighting for my life?

However, very soon I realized that the desire to get even fills us with resentment, anger, and vengefulness. I didn't like feeling that way. I didn't want to be that person. I didn't believe I deserved any of the pain; I didn't wish anything bad for those who hurt me. And I didn't want to navigate the world through the lens of toxicity. I believe that pent-up negativity can hurt us more than anything else. True healing can't begin without forgiveness, so I forgave (or thought I did) those who hurt me.

Inside my head, I was over what had transpired in 2018 and the years leading up to my illness. I healed physically after my surgery; I learned to build healthy boundaries, but I forgot that emotional healing has its own path and takes its own time.

Forgiveness is an essential ingredient in emotional healing. But saying you forgive someone isn't the same as forgiving someone. I had rushed forgiveness, and I asked myself why. Oftentimes, we are told that if you are a decent human being, you should forgive right away. I wanted to be that good person. I also felt pressured by those around me (however well-intentioned) to forgive those who had hurt me so we could talk about other things and "move on."

Honestly, I so wanted to be done with being angry and hurt. I didn't want to focus on those who hurt and disappointed me. I wanted to nourish and give my energy to those who nourished me. I wanted to end the control these offenders had on my emotions and eventually health. I wanted the heaviness in my heart and the weight on my shoulders to leave me. I didn't want to be chained to difficult memories because that stunted my inner growth.

I chose forgiveness. I figured that forgiveness was a shortcut to healing. I thought I could bypass the pain and angst if I chose forgiveness. In the *Bhagavad Gita* (16.3), Lord Krishna declares forgiveness to be a godly quality foundational for liberation and is contrasted with the anger and harshness that characterize the ungodly, who stay in bondage.

When you go through the process of truly forgiving someone, your life feels lighter. You don't bring that baggage with you everywhere you go. You don't play victim. You aren't always triggered. You feel empowered and in control.

Over the holidays, I disconnected from social media and turned inward. I didn't want to drag the achiness with me into 2021. I hired a wonderful holistic life coach (Day Singh whom I highly recommend) to seek her expert professional opinion on how to forgive. I had tried to do it on my own and clearly not succeeded. She told me that I could give myself permission to grieve and mourn what I had lost. I needn't ignore the pain I was in. She reminded me to stay patient and kind to myself.

Interestingly, the more I meditated on forgiveness for those who hurt me, the lighter I felt. I understood that while some resentments seem to vanish forever, others certainly come and go. Most importantly, I also accepted that 100 percent forgiveness is temporary. That is why you practice forgiveness and compassion on a daily basis.

In this process of letting go, detaching emotionally from my offenders, and practicing kindness and forgiveness, I received more clarity: I suspected that the people who hurt me might be struggling with mental illness themselves. They had exhibited signs over the years, but no one would dare to bring it up with them. While that doesn't excuse their behavior, I started to see them as complicated beings battling their own demons and lashing out at anyone walking in their own light and truth. I started to recognize that the problem was them, not me. Such a liberating feeling.

Trust me—forgiveness isn't a walk in the park, but a bit of practice can help us. I can tell you that forgiveness can bring you closure. You feel a sense of healthy detachment where the person who hurt you—their presence or absence; their words or silence—doesn't shake you. You remain calm in the eye of the storm. No expectations. No attachment to any outcome of engagement with them.

Forgiveness can help us reclaim ourselves.

Seven Habits We Can't Ever Forget Even After the Pandemic Is Over

> "Motivation is what gets you started. Habit is what keeps you going."
>
> —Jim Rohn

As I write this essay, I feel skeptical. Even as a raging optimist, I am unsure if this pandemic will get better, never mind over, by the end of 2020. But the pragmatic in me is nudging me to be prepared and remember the lessons we can't forget long after 2020 is done.

Our lives have been on some degree of pause for over five months now, if not more. Mother Nature gave us the chance to reevaluate how we lived and created room for growth. To each their own, but here are the 7 habits I intend to continue with long after the pandemic is over.

1. Pay attention to what we need less or more of

Most of us tend to have some sort of attachment to materialistic goods. These could be work clothes, workout attire, shoes, handbags, gadgets, cookware, groceries, or anything else. We have that extra piece in our homes because we believe we might need it. With online shopping just a click away, it's so easy to impulsively buy things without thinking. But the pandemic has taught us that there is no point in accumulation. Life happens when we are busy planning it, so spend your time with people and building memories, not hoarding items. Less is more and there is only so much we need.

2. Don't forget to be grateful

As I have been saying, in these times, it might feel like struggle to wake up every morning and find reasons to be grateful for. But gratitude is a daily practice. If you are breathing, be grateful. If you have a roof over your head, say gratitude. If your loved ones are healthy, don't forget to say thank you. If you are able to pay your bills and feed your family, have a grateful heart. If you have good health on your side, whisper gratitude.

3. Redefine self-care

Setting healthy boundaries is a radical act of self-care. Some boundaries will be around yourself; others, with people. For instance, consider rationing how much news you consume. Stop scrolling mindlessly through social media and believing that everyone has a better life than yours. Without feeling guilty, say NO to phone calls and Zoom invites if they don't nourish you, without feeling guilty. If someone wants to discuss politics and devastations around the world constantly, be okay with saying, "I'd love to talk about something else right now."

4. Power of the present moment

We live in a world where most people are either chasing tomorrow or thinking about their yesterday, because living in the present moment is considered ordinary by many. There is nothing more centering than acknowledging the power of now. Being present-minded is the key to staying healthy and happy. It helps you fight anxiety, cuts down on your worrying and rumination, and keeps you grounded and connected to yourself and everything around you. On the contrary, the tendency to get sucked into the past and/or the future can leave you perpetually worn out and feeling out of touch with yourself. Being in the present moment, or the "here and now," means that we are aware and mindful of what is happening at this very moment. We are not distracted by ruminations on the past or worries about the future but centered in the here and now. All of our attention is focused on the present moment.[13]

5. Reach Out to your community

Check in with your friends and family to see how they are doing. Everyone is coping right now. Things might seem A-Okay on the outside, but no one's life is perfect. The pandemic might have made you realize that not everyone will tell you that they are struggling. Don't bring your ego into relationships. Make it a priority to stay connected with those who matter. By the same token, it's okay to ask for help.

---

[13] https://www.myrkothum.com/what-is-the-present-moment/

6. Prioritize what's important to you

I've said it before, but it's relevant here too: put "me-time" into your daily schedule. Social distance yourself from your stress. Pavla Lokajová (writer, journalist, and corporate storyteller) has said, "I've become a mother this year, a twin mom. And somehow, it was super important for me to maintain the lifestyle I've been leading before, only with two babies attached. Pre-pandemic, I was often having coffee somewhere around the city two to three times a week, scheduling multiple calls in the naptime, and overall being available anytime to maintain a social life—and a certain picture. It was exhausting, unnecessary and unsustainable. Most of all, it was so out of tune of what I really wanted. Turned out, I wanted to do much less."

Another inspiring woman, Rachel Hills (author, producer, and founder of the New York City-based community PowerBitches) said, "I've reaffirmed that making space for creativity is more important to me than maximizing my income. During the first weeks of the coronavirus pandemic, increased family responsibilities meant I had no time to do anything but my highest yield working. Losing the time I normally spend thinking, reflecting, and creating reaffirmed how important these things are to me, and I've taken up freelance writing again after a two-year hiatus."

7. Exercising is non-negotiable

Step away from the distractions of everyday life and chores. When you feel lazy, be better than your excuses. Just 20 minutes of brisk walking can do wonders for your emotional and physical health. Some studies show that exercise can work quickly to alleviate a depressed mood in many people[14]. Besides making memories stronger, exercise can help one focus and stay on task.

---

[14] https://www.ncbi.nlm.nih.gov/pmc/articles/PMC474733/

PARTING WORDS

Epilogue

> "Be patient with yourself. Self-growth is tender; it's holy ground. There's no greater investment."
> —Stephen Covey: *The 7 Habits of Highly Effective People*

Human beings are resilient. For the most part, we bounce back from calamity with a scar and a smile. Do we have to test ourselves over and over again and stretch our boundaries to access what we can endure?

We learn to compartmentalize and move on. Many believe that survival means moving forward and not remaining entangled in the web of negative past experiences. In being brave, we start to deem that once the physical healing is over, we are mentally and emotionally ready too. This is a myth. I believe broken and unhealed people walk out into the world, pretending they are okay, and pour their pain into others' brokenness.

Sure, it's uncomfortable to sit with discomfort, or to familiarize yourself with your own darkness and tribulations. But numbing your pain, people-pleasing, and ignoring your voice are what probably got you here in the first place. It's hard to traverse through emotions and incidents that caused us pain to begin with. I say this from personal experience. But unless you experience the range of emotions—without diluting them with judgment and criticism—you can never feel whole again. You matter, and your story matters.

Stress-related disorders are the root cause of many illnesses, science has been trying to warn us. Give yourself the permission to reassess your life and purpose. Nourish and nurture yourself on a daily basis. That means observe how you feel, notice the way you navigate the world, focus on what sustains you, and pay attention to what/who depletes you. Our mind and body are related.

Talk to yourself the way you would talk to a kid you love. Show yourself the compassion you would show an elderly person. Learn to be emotionally available for yourself the way you would for your pets. Spend time in nature, listen to silence, eat well, move your body, mentally floss, i.e. meditate daily, learn to slow down, and befriend yourself.

In no way am I suggesting that you stop dreaming big and start becoming complacent. Prioritizing what's important and not chasing perfection in life, relationships, and opportunities is key to thriving.

I am not a doctor or a psychotherapist. But as an Ayurveda health counselor and a survivor of chronic illness, I have learned a few things along the way. I wrote this book to chronicle my experiences so others could benefit from it. Chronic illness and healing can feel very isolating and lonely on some days. *A Piece of Peace* is also a direct result of me wanting to take stock of my life, reminding others to focus on their wellness and healing journey, and building a community so we don't feel alone.

Glossary

Asanas: Asana is a Sanskrit term, which is often translated as "posture" or "pose." Yoga asana is the third limb of the eight-limbed path outlined in the Yoga Sutra of Patanjali—a seminal yogic text. Asanas can help slow us down and bridge any disconnections between the body, mind, and breath. Scientific research suggests that regular asana practice can lower stress, improve sleep, reduce anxiety, and help with chronic pain and circulation as well as with breathing.

Ayurveda: It is a natural and holistic system of medicine that has been practiced for more than 5,000 years and stems from the Indian subcontinent. The first aim of Ayurveda is to protect and maintain the health of the human being throughout the life span. The second aim of this science is to cure the diseases which are developed in the body of a human. Based on the idea that disease is due to an imbalance or stress in a person's consciousness, Ayurveda encourages certain lifestyle interventions and natural therapies to regain a balance between the body, mind, spirit, and the environment.

Breathwork: It refers to breathing techniques or breathing exercises performed to improve mental, physical, and emotional well-being. It teaches you to manipulate your breathing rate and depth with the goal of bringing awareness to your breath and ultimately providing the same benefits you might get from a meditative practice. Studies have found that breathwork can help lower anxiety and stress. It can also help reduce symptoms associated with insomnia, post-traumatic stress disorder, and lack of focus.

Meditation: It is a practice where an individual learns to work with the mind to bring attention and awareness so they can reach an emotionally calm and mentally stable state. Using different techniques, meditation trains your brain to observe your thoughts and feelings without judging them. Each time the mind becomes distracted, the practitioner is encouraged to come back to an object of concentration, such as the breath, a sound, an image or a philosophical or spiritual concept. There is no "right way" to meditate, meaning people can explore the different types of meditation (Loving-kindness meditation, Body scan or progressive relaxation, Mindfulness meditation, Breath awareness meditation, Kundalini yoga, Zen meditation, and Transcendental Meditation) until they find one that works for them.

Pranayama: It is a set of ancient yogic breathing techniques practiced in a specific posture and should be performed early morning on empty stomach at a well-ventilated, quite place. Breathing should be slow and rhythmic; eyes should be preferably closed to control the mind and body. Pranayama teaches us the art of extending and controlling our breath in many ways. It trains us to change the depth, rate, and pattern of breathing to achieve a certain state of meditation. Pranayama is the conscious awareness of breath. It helps to purify the blood and respiratory system. Deep breathing enriches the blood with oxygen. Large amounts of oxygen reach the brain, lungs, heart, and capillaries.

Self-care: It is the practice of taking action to protect your own well-being and happiness. It's the practice of taking an active role to improve one's health doing activities that help you to stay fit and healthy, and with enough energy to get through your work and personal commitments. Self-care is key to a good relationship with oneself and others. It is about being aware what we need to do in order to take care of ourselves and, subsequently, be able to take care of others as well. That's why your self-care must address your emotional, physical, mental, and spiritual health.

Acknowledgments

A Piece Of Peace is dear to my heart for many reasons, so I would like to express my gratitude to the many people who saw me through this book; to all those who provided support, held my hands at home and in the hospital, talked things over, read, wrote, offered comments, and assisted in my healing process.

I would like to thank my publisher, Victor R. Volkman, for enabling me to publish this book and encouraging me to write about topics that are uncomfortable and scary but need to be addressed. Doug West, the best book designer, aka mind reader an author could dream of working with. Sophy Dale for her calm personality and astute editing skills. Dr. Bob Rich for his unique thinking, astute editing, and sense of humor.

I'd also like to acknowledge Naomi Boshari *(Elephant Journal)*, Dinty W. Moore *(Brevity: A Journal of Concise Literary Nonfiction)*, Bill Miles *(Best Self Magazine)*, Barbara Bos, *(Women Writers)*, and *Cure Joy* for giving some of my essays a home in their journals. Much gratitude to all the people who shared their stories and became a part of my essays. Your words and vulnerability make us braver.

So many people have helped me through this crisis and made this book possible—from our local community to our neighbors to our friends and family. My cousins Jyotiki Agochiya, Arup Bhadra, Tulika Sinha, Nishant Deep, Tushar Sinha, Gyana Sinha, Niharika Bhasin, Prashant Sinha, and Rishi Saurabh—thank you for being the stalwart presence in our lives during our darkest hours. You held us together in the ER, in the hospital, and at home. You accompanied me to the operating room and cooked meals for me even when I couldn't eat. You cracked jokes and held my hands when I started to walk again. You didn't think twice before hopping on planes or driving long distance or staying on phone calls even when I couldn't talk. I am a better human being because of all of you.

Tony Thomas, Leah Zibulsky, Nancy Agabian, Amy Treesa Paul, Rujuta Dave, and Roy Sirengo... your support has meant the world to me. Shuchi Sethi and Vivek Yadav: Thank you for being there as my illness, this book, and life changed me. Jaya Sharan and Hena Jawaid: Thank you for offering to cancel your vacation plans and fly to NYC to help us out from Singapore and London respectively. Friends like you two are an empowering gift to me. Knowing this kind of support exists even today is all one needs on some days. Nirav Patel: you would upset me with your bad jokes, but that's what I needed to hear to feel any iota of normalcy. Thank you. Christa Nader and Anna Almiroudis... ginormous hugs for the million sweet little gestures.

My dad, who sat with me at 3 am on many nights and gave me head massages because my illness and the pain had turned me into an insomniac. For all the *kitchari* you cooked and hot water bottles you gave me on time, my body had to get better. You have taught me about courage, flexibility, adaptability, and so much more.

Above all, a big thank you to my dearest husband, Anudit. On days when I didn't believe I would make it out alive, you didn't give up on hope or on me. Thank you for your unshaken faith in my well-being, your patience with my illness, and for never letting me feel small despite what the disease had turned my body into. You made me feel beautiful on days when my body would morph into a creature from a sci-fi movie. I am writing and walking today because you believed I would heal.

Last but not least: I beg forgiveness of all those who have been with me over the course of the years and whose names I have failed to mention. You are in my gratitude prayers and good wishes.

About the Author

Sweta Srivastava Vikram (www.swetavikram.com) is an international speaker, bestselling author of 12 books, and Ayurveda and mindset coach who is committed to helping people thrive on their own terms. As a trusted source on health and wellness, most recently appearing on NBC and Radio Lifeforce and in a documentary with Dr. Deepak Chopra, Sweta has dedicated her career to writing about and teaching a more holistic approach to creativity, productivity, health, and nutrition. Her work has appeared in *The New York Times* and other publications across nine countries on three continents. Sweta is a trained yogi and certified Ayurveda health coach, is on the board of Fly Female Founders, and holds a Master's in Strategic Communications from Columbia University. Voted as "One of the Most Influential Asians of Our Times" and winner of the "Voices of the Year" award (previous recipients include Chelsea Clinton), she lives in New York City with her husband and works with clients across the globe. She also teaches yoga, meditation, and mindfulness to survivors of sexual assault and domestic violence as well as incarcerated men and women. Find her handle @swetavikram on: Twitter, Instagram, LinkedIn, and Facebook.

Bibliography

Adele, D. (2014). *The Yamas & Niyamas: Exploring Yoga's Ethical Practice*. Two Harbors: On-Word Bound Books.

Beattie, M. (2009). *The language of letting go*. Beverly Hills, CA: Phoenix Audio.

Brown, B. (2019). *Dare to lead: Brave work, tough conversations, whole hearts*.

Brown, B. (2019). *Daring greatly: How the courage to be vulnerable transforms the way we live, love, parent, and lead*.

Chödrön, P. (2003). *The Pema Chodron collection: The wisdom of no escape, Start where you are, When things fall apart*. New York: One Spirit.

Clear, J. (2018). *Atomic Habits: The life-changing million copy bestseller*. S.l.: Random House.

Devi, N. (2022). *Secret power of yoga: A woman's guide to the heart and spirit of the yoga sutras*. S.l.: Harmony Crown.

Duckworth, A. (2018). *Grit: The power of passion and perseverance*.

Gilbert, E. (2016). *Big magic*. Place of publication not identified: Bloomsbury Publishing.

Hay, L. L. (2017). *You can heal your life*.

Hay, L. L. (2012). *Heal your body: The mental causes for physical illness and the metaphysical way to overcome them*. Carlsbad, Calif: Hay House.

Harris, D. (2019). *10% happier: How I tamed the voice in my head, reduced stress without losing my edge, and found self-help that actually works : a true story*. London: Yellow Kite.

Lad, V. (2019). *Ayurvedic perspectives on selected pathologies: An anthology of essential reading from Ayurveda today*.

Lad, V., & Ayurvedic Institute. (2010). *Pranayama for self-healing: Demonstrated by Vasant Lad*. Albuquerque, N.M: Ayurvedic Institute.

Lad, V. (2006). *The complete book of Ayurvedic home remedies*. London: Piatkus.

Lad, V. (2006). *Secrets of the pulse: The ancient art of ayurvedic pulse diagnosis*. Albuquerque, N.M: Ayurvedic Press.

Kalanithi, P. (2020). *When breath becomes air*.

Manson, M. (2019). *The subtle art of not giving a f*ck: A counterintuitive approach to living a good life*.

Masters, J. (1861). *The Wynnes, or, Many men, many minds: A tale of every-day life*. London: Joseph Masters.

Moorjani, A. (2022). *Dying to be me: My journey from cancer, to near death, to true healing*. S.l.: Hay House Inc.

Nestor, J. (2021). *Breath: The new science of a lost art*. S.l.: Penguin Life.

Pole, S. (2013). *Discovering the true you with Ayurveda: How to nourish, rejuvenate and transform your life*.

Ruiz, M., Mills, J., & Ruiz, M. (2008). *The four agreements: And, the four agreements companion guide*. Thorndike, Me: Center Point Pub.

Sebastian, P. (2006). *Ayurvedic Medicine*.

Svoboda, R. (2002). *Ayurveda for women: [a guide to vitality and health]*. New Delhi: New Age Books.

Svoboda, R. (2002). *The hidden secret of Ayurveda*. Albuquerque, N.M: Ayurvedic Press.

Sincero, J. (2017). *You are a badass*.

Singer, M. (2012). *The untethered soul: The Journey Beyond Yourself*. Oakland: New Harbinger Publications.

Starzec, J. (2013). *Determination: 5k, ballet, and a spinal cord injury*.

Roach, G. M. (2020). *How Yoga Works*. Lanham: Diamond Cutter Press.

Tiwari, M. (2005). *Ayurveda: A life of balance : the complete guide to ayurvedic nutrition and body types with recipes*. New Delhi: Motilal Banarsidass Publishers.

Todd, C. (2006). *Ayurveda: The Divine Science of Life*.

Tolle, E. (2018). *The power of now: A guide to spiritual enlightenment.*

Trachtman, J (2016). *Catching what life throws at you: True stories of healing.* Seattle, WA: CreateSpace.

Index

Saris and a Single Malt is a moving collection of poems written by a daughter for and about her mother. The book spans the time from when the poet receives a phone call in New York City that her mother is in a hospital in New Delhi, to the time she carries out her mother's last rites. The poems chronicle the author's physical and emotional journey as she flies to India, tries to fight the inevitable, and succumbs to the grief of living in a motherless world. This collection will move you, astound you, and make you hug your loved ones.

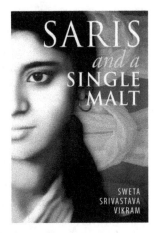

"There are few books like Saris and a Single Malt in which the loss of a mother, a homeland, and the self com together in a sustained elegy."
--JUSTEN AHREN, Director Noepe Center, Author of *A Strange Catechism*

"In life, as in poetry, one must come from the heart. Sweta Vikram has done both with touching eloquence. Her work resonates deeply within one's deepest emotional sacristy."
--SHARON KAPP, Owner & Founder, Houston Yoga & Ayurvedic Wellness Center

"Saris and a Single Malt is a fitting and delightful tribute of a writer daughter to her affectionate mother which goes deep into the minds of all children who love their moms."
--K. V. DOMINIC, English language poet, critic, short-story writer, and editor from Kerala, India

Sweta Srivastava Vikram, featured by Asian Fusion as "one of the most influential Asians of our time," is an award-winning writer, Pushcart Prize nominee, author of ten books, and a wellness practitioner. A graduate of Columbia University, Sweta performs her work, teaches creative writing workshops, and gives talks at universities and schools across the globe.

Learn more at www.swetavikram.com

From Modern History Press

A grieving daughter and abuse survivor must summon the courage to run a feminist conference, trust a man she meets over the Internet, and escape a catfishing stalker to find her power.

Ahana, a wealthy thirty-three-year-old New Delhi woman, flees the pain of her mother's death, and her dark past, by accepting a huge project in New Orleans, where she'll coordinate an annual conference to raise awareness of violence against women. Her half-Indian, half-Irish colleague and public relations guru, Rohan Brady, who helps Ahana develop her online presence, offends her prim sensibilities with his raunchy humor. She is convinced that he's a womanizer.

Meanwhile, she seeks relief from her pain in an online support group, where she makes a good friend: the mercurial Jay Dubois, who is also grieving the loss of his mother. Louisiana Catch is an emotionally immersive novel about identity, shame, and who we project ourselves to be in the world. It's a book about Ahana's unreliable instincts and her ongoing battle to deter¬mine whom to place her trust in as she, Rohan, and Jay shed layers of their identities.

"Louisiana Catch is a triumph. In Ahana, Sweta Vikram has created an unforgettable character, strong, wise, and deeply human, who'll inspire a new generation struggling to come to terms with their identity in a world of blurring identities."
--KARAN BAJAJ, New York Times bestselling author, *The Yoga of Max's Discontent*

"In Louisiana Catch, Sweta Vikram brings life to the complex human rights issue of violence against women. Through one woman's journey to make sense of her past and ultimately heal, Vikram shows us that yoga can reconnect us to ourselves, and that by empowering others, we transform our own lives."
--ZOË LEPAGE, Founder, *Exhale to Inhale*

Learn more at www.SwetaVikram.com
From Modern History Press